Practical English Language Teaching: Speaking

By Kathleen M. Bailey

Series Editor: David Nunan

Practical English Language Teaching: Speaking

Published by McGraw-Hill ESL/ELT, a business unit of The McGraw-Hill Companies, Inc. 1221 Avenue of the Americas, New York, NY 10020. Copyright © 2005 by The McGraw-Hill Companies, Inc. All rights reserved. No part of this publication may be reproduced or distributed in any form or by any means, or stored in a database or retrieval system, without the prior written consent of The McGraw-Hill Companies, Inc., including, but not limited to, in any network or other electronic storage or transmission, or broadcast for distance learning.

This book is printed on recycled, acid-free paper containing 10% post-consumer waste.

1 2 3 4 5 6 7 8 9 DOC 9 8 7 6 5 4

ISBN: 0-07-310310-1

Editorial director: *Tina B. Carver*
Executive editor: *Erik Gundersen*
Developmental editor: *Linda O'Roke*
Production managers: *Juanita Thompson, MaryRose Malley*
Cover designer: *Martini Graphic Services, Inc.*
Interior designer: *Acento Visual*
Art: *Martini Graphic Services, Inc.*
Photo credits: *Images © Getty Images, Inc./Royalty Free*

McGraw-Hill

The **McGraw·Hill** Companies

Dedication

For Les

Softly

    Playfully

        Eagerly

            Asking,

                Kindly

                    Inquiring –

                        Now

                        Gone

Acknowledgements

My publisher and I would like to thank the following individuals who reviewed the *Practical English Language Teaching* and *Practical English Language Teaching: Speaking* manuscripts at various stages of development and whose commentary was instrumental in helping us shape these professional reference volumes:

Ronald Carter, Centre for English Language Education, Department of English Studies, University of Nottingham, UK

Andy Curtis, The English School, Kingston, Ontario, Canada

Nicholas Dimmitt, Asian Institute of Technology, Pathumthani, Thailand

Fernando Fleurquin, ALIANZA, Montevideo, Uruguay

Donald Freeman, School for International Training, Brattleboro, Vermont, USA

Marc Helgesen, Miyagi Gakuin Women's University, Sendai, Japan

Caroline Linse, Sookmyung University, Seoul, Korea

Donald Occhiuzzo, World Learning/School for International Training; formerly of Alumni, São Paulo, Brazil

Betsy Parrish, Hamline University, St. Paul, Minnesota, USA

Kathy Weed, Editor, *TESOL's Essential Teacher*, Geneva, Switzerland.

In addition, David Nunan, the series editor, gave me helpful feedback on the draft as well as clear guidelines with which to work and a strong sense of vision about the series as a whole.

My critical buddy, **Andy Curtis**, provided encouragement, asked great questions, and suggested classroom examples to illustrate some of the ideas in my draft. He also pointed out differences among British, Canadian, and American varieties of English. As a peer reviewer, Andy is the best!

The members of the editorial team at McGraw-Hill ESL/ELT–**Erik Gundersen**, **Linda O'Roke**, and **David Averbach**.

Here at the Monterey Institute of International Studies, my friend and assistant, **Jeff Mattison**, helped with word processing, Web searches, proofreading, bibliography checks, and library research. His work with me was supported in part by a faculty development grant from **Joseph** and **Sheila Marks**, long-term supporters of the Monterey Institute.

Some extracts in Chapter 4 are based on data collected by **Renee Jourdenais** and transcribed by **Cicely Rude**. An extract in Chapter 5 was collected and transcribed by **Mandy Deal**. I appreciate their permission to use these transcripts.

Finally, as the submission deadline drew near, my friends **Jessica Massie** and **Bethany Alling** helped with word processing, assembling, and checking the manuscript. My dad, **Henry McMillan**, worked and reworked the logic puzzle in Chapter 3.

Thank you all so much! Kathi Bailey

Table of Contents

Foreword

Vision and purpose

The *Practical English Language Teaching* series is designed for practicing teachers, or teachers in preparation who may or may not have formal training in second and foreign language teaching methodology. The core volume in this series, *Practical English Language Teaching*, provides an overall introduction to key aspects of language teaching methodology in an accessible yet not trivial way. The purpose of this book is to explore the teaching of speaking in greater depth than was possible in the core volume, while at the same time remaining both comprehensive and accessible.

Features

- A clear orientation to the teaching of speaking, including an historical overview and an introduction to major approaches and analyses that have informed pedagogy.
- A detailed treatment of the teaching of speaking at beginning, intermediate, and advanced levels, providing practical techniques for teaching and assessing speaking and pronunciation at each of these levels.
- Reflection questions inviting readers to think about critical issues in language teaching and Action tasks requiring readers to apply the ideas, principles, and techniques to the teaching of speaking and pronunciation in their own situation.
- A great deal of practical illustration from a wide range of textbooks and extracts from authentic classroom interaction.
- A "key issues" chapter that provides suggestions for dealing with large, multi-level classes, introducing technology, and catering to different learning styles and strategies.
- Suggestions for books, articles, and Websites offering resources for additional up-to-date information.
- An expansive glossary that offers short and straightforward definitions of core language teaching terms.

Audience

As with the overview volume, this book is designed for both experienced and novice teachers. It should also be of value to those who are about to join the profession. It will update the experienced teacher on current theoretical and practical approaches to teaching speaking. The novice teacher will find step-by-step guidance on the practice of language teaching.

Overview

Chapter 1

The first chapter provides an orientation and historical overview of the teaching of speaking. The chapter also introduces key principles for teaching and assessing speaking.

Chapters 2–4

Chapters 2–4 introduce you to the teaching of speaking to beginning, intermediate, and advanced students respectively. Each chapter follows the format below.

Chapter 5

The final chapter explores key issues including the teaching of speaking and pronunciation in large, multi-level classes, working with learners who have different learning styles and strategies, responding to learners' errors, and using technology.

Chapter structure for Chapters 2–4

Goals: Summarizes what you should know and be able to do after having read the chapter and completed the Reflection and Action tasks.

Introduction: Gives an overview of the chapter.

Syllabus design issues: Outlines the speaking issues that are relevant at different levels, and the concerns that inform syllabus design.

Principles for teaching speaking: Appropriate principles for teaching speaking at different levels are introduced, discussed, and illustrated.

Tasks and materials: Describes and illustrates techniques and exercises for teaching speaking and pronunciation at each level.

Assessing speaking: Introduces practical techniques for assessing learners in the classroom.

Conclusion: Reviews the goals of the chapter and how they were discussed within the chapter.

Further readings: Lists articles or books to enhance your knowledge about teaching speaking and pronunciation.

Helpful Web sites: Provides ideas for Web resources for teaching speaking and pronunciation.

Chapter **One**

What is speaking?

1. Introduction

This chapter will explore the fundamental concept of speaking and its components, including the important subtopic of pronunciation. In the first part of the chapter, we will answer the question, "What is speaking?" Next, in Section 3, we will examine different approaches to teaching speaking. Then, in Section 4, we will study a model of the various components that must come into play when we are speaking in a new language. In the process we will review some differences between spoken and written language. In Section 5, we will look at some important issues about teaching speaking, including a quick overview of the main teaching methods that have been used over the years. Finally, we will consider the vexing question of how learners' speaking skills should be assessed.

2. What is speaking?

In this section, we will consider what we mean by "speaking." In language teaching we often talk about the four language skills (speaking, listening, reading, and writing) in terms of their direction and modality. Language generated by the learners (in either speech or writing) is considered **productive**, and language directed at the learners (in reading or listening) is known as **receptive** language (Savignon, 1991). **Modality** refers to the medium of the language (whether it is aural/oral or written). Thus, **speaking** is the productive, oral skill.

Speaking consists of producing systematic verbal utterances to convey meaning. (**Utterances** are simply things people say.) Speaking is "an interactive process of constructing meaning that involves producing and receiving and processing information" (Florez, 1999, p. 1). It is "often spontaneous, open-ended, and evolving" (ibid., p. 1), but it is not completely unpredictable.

Speaking is such a fundamental human behavior that we don't stop to analyze it unless there is something noticeable about it. For example, if a person is experiencing a speech pathology (if a person stutters or if his speech is impaired due to a stroke or a head injury), we may realize that the speech is atypical. Likewise, if someone is a particularly effective or lucid speaker, we may notice that her speech is atypical in a noteworthy sense. What we fail to notice on a daily basis, however, are the myriad physical, mental, psychological, social, and cultural factors that must all work together when we speak. It is even a more impressive feat when we hear someone speaking effectively in a second or foreign language.

3. Approaches to speaking

For many years, language teaching was seen as helping learners develop **linguistic competence**–that is, helping students master the sounds, words, and grammar patterns of English. The idea was that by studying the bits and pieces of a language, students could eventually put them all together and communicate.

In the 1970s and 1980s, however, our understanding of language learning experienced a significant shift in focus. This shift was influenced by international developments in linguistics, curricula, and pedagogy, as well as by sociolinguistic research (primarily in Australia, Canada, New Zealand, the United Kingdom, and the U.S.). In addition, the numbers of refugees and immigrants resettling in English-speaking countries made linguists and language teachers realize that developing linguistic competence alone was not enough to be able to speak English well and get along in society.

In the mid-1970s the notion of linguistic competence came to be viewed as a component of the broader idea of **communicative competence** "the ability of language learners to interact with other speakers, to make meaning, as distinct from their ability to perform on discrete-point tests of grammatical knowledge" (Savignon, 1991, p. 264). Being communicatively competent "requires an understanding of sociocultural contexts of language use" (ibid., p. 267).

There are several important models of communicative competence (see especially Bachman, 1990, and Canale and Swain, 1980), all of which include some form of **sociolinguistic competence**, or the ability to use language appropriately in various contexts. Sociolinguistic competence involves **register** (degrees of formality and informality), appropriate word choice, **style shifting**, and politeness strategies.

Another important element of communicative competence is **strategic competence**. In terms of speaking, this is the learner's ability to use language strategies to compensate for gaps in skills and knowledge. For example, if you don't know a word you need to express your meaning, what strategies can you use to make your point?

A fourth component of communicative competence is **discourse competence**, "how sentence elements are tied together," which includes both cohesion and coherence (Lazaraton, 2001, p. 104). **Cohesion** is "the grammatical and/or lexical relationship between the different parts of a sentence" (Richards, Platt, and Weber, 1985, p. 45). Cohesion includes reference, repetition, synonyms, and so on. In contrast, **coherence** involves "how texts are constructed" (Lazaraton, 2001, p. 104; see also Bachman, 1990, pp. 84–102, and Douglas, 2000, pp. 25–29). Let's consider the following conversation as an illustration.

> **Extract 1**
>
> *Jeff:* Hey, Lindsey, how's it going?
>
> *Lindsey:* Wow! I just had a test and it was really hard!
>
> *Jeff:* Oh, what was the test about?
>
> *Lindsey:* Statistics! All those formulas are so confusing!
>
> *Jeff:* Yeah, I don't like that stuff either.

In this brief conversation, there are several examples of cohesion. In Lindsey's first turn the pronoun *it* refers to the test she has just mentioned. In Jeff's second turn, he repeats the word *test.* In Lindsey's second turn, the words *statistics* and *formulas* are synonymous. Finally, in Jeff's last turn "that stuff" refers to *statistics* and *formulas.* All these devices make the conversation cohesive.

Coherence also has to do with "the relationships which link the meanings of utterance in a discourse" (Richards, Platt, and Weber, 1985, p. 45). However, coherence often involves the speakers' background knowledge. For example, the following exchange is coherent because the two people know that the two events are scheduled at the same time:

> **Extract 2**
>
> *Person 1:* Going to the review session?
>
> *Person 2:* Rugby practice.

Both cohesion and coherence contribute to discourse competence. For people speaking in a new language, the specific linguistic elements that make speech cohesive can be especially demanding to produce during the pressure of a conversation.

Reflection

Think about someone you know who is truly bilingual or multilingual who can function effectively and apparently effortlessly in two or more languages. Can you think of examples of the four components of communicative competence in that person's speech?

I have a friend named Lillian, who is a native speaker of Cantonese. She is a fully-competent bilingual who regularly demonstrates all four components of communicative competence when she speaks. In terms of her linguistic competence, she has very good pronunciation, a wide vocabulary, and excellent mastery of English grammar rules. She also can appropriately engage in many different types of speaking, from a casual conversation to giving a formal conference presentation to a large audience of strangers. Her speech displays both cohesion and coherence, so she demonstrates her discourse competence as well. If she needs to use an unfamiliar word or structure, she uses her strategic competence and finds a way to convey her meaning.

These four components of communicative competence have several practical implications for EFL and ESL teachers. Since communicative competence is a multifaceted construct, it is important for teachers to understand the complexities learners face when they are speaking English.

One of those complexities is balancing fluency and accuracy. A proficient speaker is both fluent and accurate. **Accuracy** in this context refers to the ability to speak properly–that is, selecting the correct words and expressions to convey the intended meaning, as well as using the grammatical patterns of English. **Fluency**, on the other hand, is the capacity to speak fluidly, confidently, and at a rate consistent with the norms of the relevant native speech community. (We will revisit the concepts of fluency and accuracy in Chapter 4.)

An important concept for teachers to understand is that while students are at the beginning and intermediate levels of language learning, that is, while they are still developing their proficiency, fluency and accuracy often work against each other. Before grammar rules become automatic and while learners are still acquiring essential vocabulary items, applying the rules and searching one's memory for the right words can be laborious mental processes, which slow the learners' speech and make them seem dysfluent. Likewise, language learners can sometimes speak quickly, without hesitating to apply the rules they have learned, but doing so may decrease their accuracy (that is, the number of errors they make in speaking may increase).

Reflection

Think about a time when you yourself were studying a new language. What was more important to you—fluency or accuracy? Did you consistently try to combine the two? Or did your focus at the time depend on the context in which you were speaking?

An important concept to keep in mind is that people use language in recognizable ways to get things done. There are many, many **"speech acts"** (or **functions**) in any language, and it is important that students learn the appropriate ways to accomplish their goals when they are speaking. Some important speech acts in English include thanking, requesting information, apologizing, refusing, warning, complimenting, directing, complaining, and so on.

One interesting issue in teaching and learning speech acts is that there is no one-to-one form/meaning correspondence. The same utterance can be used to mean more than one thing, and this duality can be the source of some confusion. For example, many years ago, my husband and I were packing our gear for a camping trip. He asked me, "Did you pack the silverware?" and I said no. That evening, after driving for several hours, we set up camp, and cooked a meal. When we sat down to eat, we discovered that we had no eating utensils. I had interpreted his question as a request for information, and assumed that he would pack the silverware. He had intended his question as a directive, reminding me that I should pack the silverware.

Likewise, there are many ways to accomplish the same goal in speaking English—in other words, different forms can be used to accomplish the same speech act. Think about the following utterances:

1. It's cold in here!
2. Aren't you forgetting something?
3. Hey, how about closing the door?

All of these utterances are directives used to try to get someone to close a door to a room. These sentences would be spoken by someone inside the room to the person who had left the door open. Understanding these utterances and acting on them appropriately, however, depends on the context in which they are spoken. The context apparently involves two (or more) people, a room with an open door, and a cold day. But would a low-level employee make any of these statements to a company president? Almost certainly not. These directives are all very casual—in fact, quite informal—and would probably only be said by social equals who know one another quite well (or by someone who has no concern for politeness constraints, or who has different expectations about politeness).

There are many ways of making spoken utterances more or less polite. The various linguistic means of softening a message are known as **mitigation**. This "softening" can be accomplished through pronunciation of words, phrases, clauses, or entire utterances.

What are the specific differences among the following utterances?

1. Pack the silverware.
2. Please pack the silverware.
3. Would you please pack the silverware?
4. I'd appreciate it if you would please pack the silverware.

What are the mitigating effects of the additions made to each subsequent utterance?

As you can see, these utterances get increasingly longer as words are added. The basic proposition remains the same: the speaker wants the listener to pack the silverware. What changes then?

In the first utterance, we have just the bare imperative, or command. Syntactically it consists of the verb *(pack)* and the direct object *(the silverware)*. In the second utterance, only the politeness marker, *please*, has been added. In the third, the basic proposition (the speaker wants the hearer to pack the silverware) and the politeness markers are embedded in a question form: "Would you...?" Finally, in the fourth utterance, that entire question has been embedded in the additional statement, "I'd appreciate it if...." Each of these changes has the effect of softening, or mitigating, the directness of the request.

This exercise reminds us that the same basic proposition can be conveyed in many different ways. As people learn to speak English, they must develop their repertoires for expressing themselves appropriately in various situations.

4. Speaking in action

Figure 1 on page 8, which I think of as van Lier's (1995) pyramid, is a "picture" of the components of spoken language. The left column lists four traditional areas of linguistic analysis (which teachers must understand), and the center column labels the units of spoken language (which learners must master). These units are often referred to as the "levels" of language. They must all work together, simultaneously, when learners speak English. We will use this pyramid as a tool for exploring the components of spoken English that we, as teachers, must understand in order to help our learners.

Reflection

Study the labels in Figure 1 and circle any that are unfamiliar to you. Try to guess at their meanings and see if your predictions are supported in the paragraphs explaining the figure.

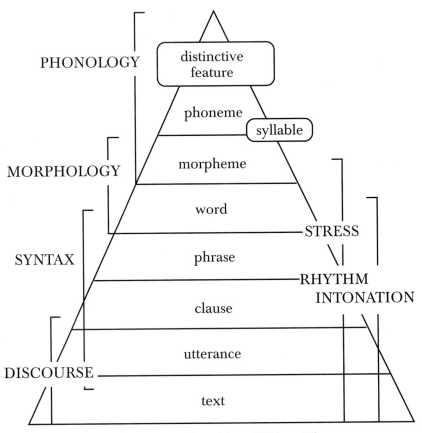

Figure 1 Units of Language (van Lier, 1995, p. 15)

Let's start with the pyramid's base. Although the word **text** is often associated in the layperson's mind with written language, texts can be either written or spoken. Here the term refers to stretches of language of an undetermined length. Spoken texts consist of utterances: things that people say. In speech, an utterance is not always a complete grammatical sentence, as sentences are used in writing. For example, if two close friends are talking about what to eat, we might hear a conversation that goes something like this:

> **Extract 3**
>
> **Person 1:** *Hungry?*
>
> **Person 2:** *Yep.*
>
> **Person 1:** *Pizza?*
>
> **Person 2:** *Nope.*
>
> **Person 1:** *Mexican?*
>
> **Person 2:** *Mmmhm, nah.*
>
> **Person 1:** *Chinese?*
>
> **Person 2:** *Maybe.*
>
> **Person 1:** *Sushi!*
>
> **Person 2:** *Yeah!*

None of these utterances is a complete sentence, but the conversation is typical of casual spoken language and it makes sense to us. It is a text consisting of utterances that are not sentences. (You can use such a conversation as speaking practice in class: have students see how long they can sustain a conversation that consists of only one-word utterances.)

Reflection

Listen to people speaking English on a bus or a train, in a restaurant, in a store—in any public place where people are talking normally and where it is not inappropriate for you to listen to them. Do they speak in complete grammatical sentences, or do they use utterances that are not complete sentences?

To continue our exploration of the next level in van Lier's pyramid (page 8), a **clause** consists of at least two words (usually more) that contain a grammatical subject and a verb marked for tense (that is, a verb that is not in its infinitive or "bare" form). **Independent clauses** are full sentences that can stand alone in written discourse ("Anna was cooking dinner"), while **dependent clauses** cannot ("While Anna was cooking dinner..."). A dependent clause must be attached to an independent clause to be complete. ("While Anna was cooking dinner, the telephone rang.")

The next level, a **phrase**, consists of two or more words that function as a unit, but unlike clauses, they do not have a subject or a verb marked for tense. There are several kinds of phrases, including prepositional phrases ("in the hospital" or "after school"), noun phrases ("a big black cat" or "the five-story building"), and infinitive phrases ("to drive" or "to move up"). Clauses and phrases are quite commonly used as utterances when we are speaking, but they do not typically appear alone in formal writing (unless the author is representing speech). Thus, both clauses and phrases can be utterances.

As we saw in the conversation about what to eat, individual words, the next level in the pyramid, can also function as utterances. Words are called **free morphemes**. These are units of language that can stand on their own and convey meaning *(baby, application, seldom)*. In contrast, **bound morphemes** do not appear alone. They are always connected to words. Both prefixes, such as *inter-* or *pre-*, and suffixes, such as *–ing* or *–s* or *-ed* are bound morphemes. You may have noticed that during the pressure of speaking, it can be difficult for English learners to use bound morphemes–especially suffixes–consistently. This problem is particularly true if the learner's native language doesn't use these kinds of morphemes as markers that convey grammatical meaning (for instance Cantonese or Mandarin).

The top most levels of the pyramid are very important in speaking–especially in developing intelligible pronunciation. A **phoneme** is a divisible unit of sound that distinguishes meaning. In writing about phonemes, we usually set them off with slashes to distinguish phonemes from letters. Phonemes can be either consonants (like /p/ or /b/ in the words *pear* and *bear*) or vowels (like /I/ and /æ/ in *hit* and *hat*). The sounds that function as phonemes differ somewhat from one language to another. Some of the sounds that are common in English are unusual in other languages, and can be quite challenging for learners to pronounce. For example, the two English "th" sounds (as in *think* and *the*) are not very common in the phonemic inventory of the world's languages, but they are pervasive in English. Students may replace or approximate these "th" sounds with /s/ or /z/ or /d/ or /t/ instead. This kind of substitution is part of what creates a foreign accent.

Figure 1 is helpful but in real conversations, of course, these divisions of discourse are not as neat as the diagram makes them seem. Consider the command, "Stop!" This is a single word (in fact, a single free morpheme) consisting of four segmental phonemes. It serves as a warning (a particular speech act). It is an utterance, and therefore, a type of spoken text. (It can also be a complete written text, for example on a traffic sign.) So keep in mind that a discourse can consist of texts of any length.

You can see that in the top levels of Figure 1 (page 8), **syllable** overlaps the levels of morphemes and phonemes. This image represents the fact that a syllable can consist of a morpheme or simply one or more phonemes. Many words, such as *stop,* consist of only one syllable.

The syllable structure of a language is either **open** (ending with a vowel) or **closed** (ending with a consonant). Many languages use the open syllable structure, in which a syllable consists of just a vowel (V), or of a consonant (C) followed by a vowel (V). Spoken English, in contrast, allows both open syllables (C-V or just V) and closed syllables (C-V-C, or simply V-C), as well as consonant clusters, where two or more consonants occur in sequence (as in the words *stretched* or *jumped*). For this reason, learners' spoken English often sounds ungrammatical to native speakers. For instance, learners whose native language is Vietnamese may omit word-final consonants when speaking English. Doing so eliminates sounds that convey important linguistic information, such as plurality, possession, or tense.

Reflection

Think about a second or foreign language you have studied. (Of course, that could be English if it is not your native language. If you have not learned a new language, think about one that you have often heard spoken.) Does that language use primarily open syllables or closed syllables? Or does it permit both open and closed syllables? Think particularly about the last syllable of many common words.

Action

Now test your hypothesis about the syllable structure of this particular language. Ask someone you know well, who is a native speaker or a very advanced speaker of that language, whether the following are syllables that appear (or are even possible) in speaking that language. Circle those that are possible or actual syllables in that language.

-tion	-sa	-stand	-fe
-ding	-po	-tent	-ti
-tles	-ly	-cal	-ku

What patterns do you notice in your data? Does this language permit open syllables, closed syllables, or both?

Consonants and vowels are called **segmental phonemes**, because they can be segmented and moved around. Have you ever produced a "slip of the tongue," because you had switched two phonemes? One typical speaking glitch is called a **spoonerism**, after Dr. Spooner, a famous British orator who taught at Oxford University in the Victorian era. Unfortunately, Dr. Spooner would sometimes switch his segmental phonemes and say things like "the queer old dean" when he meant to say "the dear old queen." He did this so often that the phenomenon came to be called "spoonerisms." The fact that sounds can be switched in this way provides linguistic evidence that phonemes are in fact segmented, independent units.

How do the segmental phonemes relate to the syllable structure of English? Sometimes a spoken syllable is just one phoneme (/o/ in *okay*). But syllables are also made up of combined sounds (the second syllable of *okay*), and of both free and bound morphemes. For instance, the free morpheme *hit* consists of three phonemes but only one syllable. The dictionary shows that the word *disheartened* is pronounced as /dis_hár-tnd/. But if we analyze it further, we find that it has three syllables, four morphemes (*dis* + *heart* + *en* + *ed*), and nine phonemes (/d/ /I/ /s/ /h/ /a/ /r/ /t/ /n/ /d/). To add to the difficulty, English has was is called a "low phoneme-grapheme correspondence." (A **grapheme** is a written unit of language.) In other words, the way English is written doesn't always match the way words are pronounced in modern English. The last two E's of *disheartened,* for instance, are not spoken aloud as we say the word. If they were, *disheartened* would have four syllables.

The **distinctive feature** is an even smaller unit of spoken language. This concept is extremely important in teaching pronunciation. It relates to how and where in the mouth a sound is produced. These minute contrasts contribute to learners' accents. For example, the distinctive feature that makes /b/ and /p/ separate phonemes in English is **voicing**. When /b/ is pronounced the vocal cords are vibrating, but when /p/ is pronounced, they are not. For learners whose language does not have this contrast (Arabic, for example), failure to master this distinction can lead to misunderstandings. (One of my Egyptian students once told me that he had had "green bee soup" for lunch!)

Sometimes we can see evidence of the distinctive features of a learner's first language in his writing. One of my advanced writing students, a native speaker of Chinese, was writing a composition about a beautiful photograph. He wrote, "The scene is so lovely it reaches out and craps your eyes." This student was not trying to be offensive. He was unknowingly processing English spelling through the sound system of his native language. The /g/, /b/ and /z/ in the word *grabs* /græbz/ had all been changed from voiced segmental phonemes to their voiceless counterparts as he wrote.

Reflection

Think about learners you have taught, or about the students you hope to teach in the future (for instance, speakers of Spanish, Chinese, Thai, or Russian). What are the typical features you associate with their accents as they are speaking English? What are the characteristics of their spoken English that allow you to recognize it as being produced by a Spanish speaker, or a Chinese speaker, or someone whose first language is Thai or Russian?

The three other labels in Figure 1 (page 8)—stress, rhythm, and intonation—represent some **suprasegmental phonemes**. The word *suprasegmental* is used because these phonemes (including pitch and stress) carry meaning differences "above" the segmental phonemes when we speak. For instance, the sentence "I am leaving now" can convey at least four different meanings, depending on where the stress is placed. The differences are related to the context where the utterances occur. Consider these interpretations:

> *I* am leaving now. (You may be staying here, but I choose to go.)
> I *am* leaving now. (You may assert that I'm staying, but I insist that I am going.)
> I am *leaving* now. (I insist that I am going, rather than staying.)
> I am leaving *now.* (I am not waiting any longer.)

Read the four sentences above to two or three friends who are native or proficient speakers of English. First, ask your friends to listen as you read all four sentences. (Be sure to stress the words that are printed in boldface.) Next, read one sentence at a time and have your friends explain the meaning differences that they infer from just the changes in the stress on the four different words. Do their explanations match the interpretations given above? (You can do this activity with your students too.)

Intonation is another very important suprasegmental phoneme. **Intonation** is the relative rise and fall of the pitch in an utterance. Intonation helps us recognize questions ("It's ten o'clock" versus "It's ten o'clock?"). Intonation also helps us detect speaker attitudes, such as surprise, sarcasm, or disbelief.

Read the sentence "He's a brain surgeon" aloud to a friend. First, read it simply as a statement of fact. Have your friend repeat this sentence. Next, ask your friend to say this same sentence as if she is surprised. Next, have her say it (using exactly the same words in the same order) as though she doesn't believe the statement—that is, she is incredulous. Finally, have her say, "He's a brain surgeon" very sarcastically—as a way of indicating that a person is not particularly intelligent. How do the intonation contours change as the speaker changes her intended meaning?

The suprasegmental and segmental phonemes are very important in speaking English. First of all, since these phonemes carry meaning, speakers who mispronounce them can be misunderstood. Second, production problems can convey unintended meanings. Research has shown that second-language speakers can be misunderstood and even receive poor job evaluations because of their misuse of the English suprasegmentals (Gumperz & Tannen, 1979). We will return to this issue in Chapter 4.

When we teach speaking, it is important to remember that spoken and written English differ in many ways (van Lier, 1995). Speech is received auditorially, whereas writing is received visually. As a result, the spoken message is temporary and its reception by the listener is usually immediate. In contrast, written language is permanent, and reception by the learner typically occurs some time after the text was generated (sometimes even centuries later). Meaning in spoken English is conveyed in part through the suprasegmental phonemes (including rhythm, stress, pitch, and intonation), whereas punctuation marks and type fonts convey such information in writing.

Another feature of spoken language is **reduced speech**—the tendency of sounds to blend together, especially in casual conversation. For instance, the words "going to" may sound like "gonna" when we are speaking quickly. Such reductions are not just "sloppy speech" resulting from the speaker's laziness or carelessness. They are actually systematic, rule-governed variants that are natural in spoken English.

Reflection

Consider the following pairs of sentences and utterances. Which member of each pair seems more like casual speech, and which seems more like written language? What are the specific differences between the two items in each pair?

Set 1
a. Hello. What are you doing?
b. Hey, what're yuh doin'?

Set 2
a. I do not know.
b. I dunno.

Set 3
a. Give me a second, would you?
b. Gimme a sec, wouldja?

Action

Most people agree that in the three different pairs of utterances in the Reflection box above, the first member of each pair seems more formal and may be a written version of speech. The second member of each pair seems more like casual speech. What characteristics do you recognize as "speech-like" here (realizing, of course, that these are written renditions of speech)? Ask a classmate or colleague these same questions and compare your ideas.

Reflection

Consider the following pairs of utterances. Which member of each pair seems more like natural, casual speech, and which seems more like written language? What are the specific differences between the two items in each pair?

Set 1
a. I'm going to the store. (Grammatical)
b. I'm gonna the store. (Ungrammatical)

Set 2
a. I'm going to go swimming. (Grammatical)
b. I'm gonna go swimming. (Grammatical)

Set 3
a. Going to the game tonight? (Grammatical)
b. Gonna the game tonight? (Ungrammatical)

Set 4
a. I'm going to go dancing tonight. (Grammatical)
b. I'm gonna go dancing tonight. (Grammatical)

Why are items 1-b and 3-b ungrammatical while items 2-b and 4-b are grammatical (although casual)? (Hint: Look at the two different uses of "to" in the phrase "going to" in these utterances. The key is what follows the "to" in each case.)

Do you see the pattern? If you carefully consider sentences 2-a and 4-a where *going to* is still pronounced quickly, *going* and *to* blend together to form *gonna*. In contrast, in sentences 1-a and 3-a, *to* is used in the prepositional phrases *to the store* and *to the game*. In these contexts, the /t/ is not reduced. This example illustrates that the sounds system of English sometimes interacts with its grammatical features.

Speaking English (or any other new language) can be particularly diffi-cult, because unlike reading or writing, speaking happens in "real time." In other words, the **interlocutor** (the person we are talking to) is listening and waiting to take his or her own turn to speak right then. "This means that a variety of demands are in place at once: monitoring and understanding the other speaker(s), thinking about one's own contribution, producing its effect, and so on" (Lazaraton, 2001, p. 103). In addition, except in recorded speech, verbal interaction typically involves immediate feedback from one's inter-locutor, while feedback to the authors of written texts may be delayed or non-existent. Finally, because spoken communication occurs in real time, the opportunities for planning and editing output are limited, while in most writ-ten communication, the message originator has time for planning, editing, and revision.

5. Teaching speaking

In this section, we look briefly at some different approaches that have been used over the years to teach languages. Although there are many dif-ferent methods of language teaching, three methods have dominated lan-guage teaching in the past sixty years. In this section, we will first briefly review each method, focusing specifically on how speaking is taught.

The Grammar-translation Method

In the **Grammar-translation Method**, students are taught to analyze grammar and to translate (usually in writing) from one language to another. Historically, the main goal of this method has been for students to read the literature of a particular culture. According to Richards and Rodgers (1986, pp. 3–4), the characteristics of the Grammar-translation Method are that (1) it focuses on reading and writing; (2) the vocabulary studied is determined by the reading texts; (3) "the sentence is the basic unit of teaching and language practice" (ibid., p. 4); (4) the primary emphasis is on accuracy; (5) teaching is deductive (i.e., grammar rules are presented and then practiced through translating); and (6) the medium of instruction is typically the students' native language.

The Grammar-translation Method does not really prepare students to speak English, so it is not entirely appropriate for students who want to improve their speaking skills. In fact, in the Grammar-translation Method, students "developed an intellectual understanding of language struc-ture and maybe the ability to read, but instead of gaining oral fluency they suffered from what could be described as second language mutism" (Hammerly, 1991, p. 1). The method is not consistent with the goals of increasing English learners' fluency, oral production, or communicative competence. In grammar-translation lessons, speaking consists largely of reading translations aloud or doing grammar exercises orally. There are few opportunities for expressing original thoughts or personal needs and feelings in English.

The Direct Method and Audiolingualism

Unlike the Grammar-translation Method's emphasis on written text, the **Direct Method** focused on "everyday vocabulary and sentences" (Richards and Rodgers, 1986, p. 9), and lessons were conducted entirely in the **target language**—the language the students are trying to learn. The Direct Method dominated English language instruction in the United States for many years.

The Direct Method emphasized speaking in that "new teaching points were introduced orally" (Richards and Rodgers, 1986, p. 10), rather than in writing. Also, lessons emphasized speaking and listening, which were practiced "in a carefully graded progression organized around question-and-answer exchanges between teachers and students" (Richards and Rodgers, 1986, p. 10). Many people became familiar with this approach since it was used by the Berlitz language schools.

The Direct Method strongly influenced the development of the **Audiolingual Method**. In audiolingualism, speaking is taught by having students repeat sentences and recite memorized dialogues from the textbook. Repetition drills—a hallmark of the Audiolingual Method—are designed to familiarize students with the sounds and structural patterns of the language. Lessons followed the sequence of presentation, practice, and production (see Nunan, 2003). The assumption underpinning the Audiolingual Method is that students learn to speak by practicing grammatical structures until producing those structures has become automatic. When this happens, it is hoped that the learners will be able to carry on conversations. As a result, "teaching oral language was thought to require no more than engineering the repeated oral production of structures...concentrating on the development of grammatical and phonological accuracy combined with fluency" (Bygate, 2001, p. 15).

The behaviorist notion of good habit formation is the theory behind the Audiolingual Method. This theory suggests that for learners to form good habits, language lessons must involve frequent repetition and correction. Teachers treat spoken errors quickly, in hopes of preventing students from forming bad habits. If errors are left untreated, it is thought, both the speaker and the other students in class might internalize those erroneous forms. In audiolingual lessons, intense repetition and practice are used to establish good speaking habits to the point that they are fluent and automatic, so the learners don't have to stop and think about how to form an utterance while they are speaking.

The language laboratory is the main technological component of the Audiolingual Method. Students are expected to spend time in the lab, listening to audiotapes of native speakers talking in scripted, rehearsed dialogues, which embody the structures and vocabulary items the learners are studying in class. The taped speech samples students hear in the lab are carefully articulated and highly sanitized. They are not usually realistic samples of the English learners would hear on the street. Nor are they necessarily good models of how learners themselves should try to speak to sound natural.

In addition, when learners do speak in the lab, it is often to repeat after the tape-recorded voice, with little or no opportunity for constructing their ideas in English or expressing their own intended meaning. The Audiolingual Method stressed oral skills but "speech production was tightly controlled in order to reinforce correct habit formation of linguistic rules" (Lazaraton, 2001, p. 103). This sort of rigidly controlled practice does not necessarily prepare learners for the spontaneous, fluid interaction that occurs outside the English classroom.

Audiolingualism eventually decreased in popularity because "the results obtained from classroom practice were disappointing" in several ways (Ellis, 1990, p. 29). Many learners thought the pattern practice and audiolingual drills were boring and lost interest in language learning. Students, perhaps especially adult learners, often felt hampered because the method down-played the explicit teaching of grammar rules. In addition, memorizing patterns "did not lead to fluent and effective communication in real-life situations" (ibid., p. 30).

Communicative Language Teaching

During the 1970s and 1980s, language acquisition research (and dissatisfaction with the Audiolingual Method) made teachers, materials developers, and curriculum designers reconsider some long-standing beliefs about how people learn languages. Apparently people don't learn the pieces of the language and then put them together to make conversations. Instead, infants acquiring their first language and people acquiring second languages seem to learn the components of language through interaction with other people. (For summaries of research on interaction and language learning, see Ellis, 1990; Gass, 1997; and Larsen-Freeman & Long, 1991.) This realization has several interesting implications for us as teachers, the most important being that if people learn languages by interacting, then students should interact during English lessons. As a result, **Communicative Language Teaching** arose.

In some language teaching methods, such as **Total Physical Response** (Asher, Kusodo, and de la Torre, 1993), beginning learners undergo a period of listening to English before they begin to speak it. In such methods, the focus is on input-based activities. For instance, in Total Physical Response, learners initially respond physically to spoken commands from the teacher, rather than speaking themselves. (We will learn more about this method in Chapter 2.)

In contrast, Communicative Language Teaching, particularly from the high beginning to more advanced levels, features more interaction-based activities, such as role-plays and **information gap tasks** (activities in which learners must use English to convey information known to them but not to their speaking partners). Pairwork and groupwork are typical organizational features of interaction-based lessons in Communicative Language Teaching.

Reflection

With a partner, make a list of advantages and disadvantages of learning to speak when the teacher is using the Grammar-translation Method, the Audiolingual Method, or Communicative Language Teaching. As a learner, which method do you prefer? As a teacher, which method do you prefer? Why?

You will recall from our discussion of communicative competence (p. 3) that strategic competence was one of its four components. In Communicative Language Teaching, teachers help learners develop their communicative strategies.

Communication strategies

When we speak, and especially perhaps when we speak in a foreign language, there are times when we wish to say something, but we don't have the words or the grammatical structures to say it. Under these circumstances, people often use **communication strategies**–verbal and/or nonverbal procedures for compensating for gaps in speaking competence.

Reflection

Think about a time when you were trying to make yourself understood in your second language or in a foreign language. What did you do, verbally and nonverbally, to convey your ideas when you lacked the vocabulary and/or the grammatical structures you needed? Were you successful at being understood? Why or why not?

In the early 1980s, applied linguists began systematically studying English learners' uses of communication strategies. A number of important strategies were documented, and soon teachers and syllabus designers began to incorporate the teaching of communication strategies in speaking classes. The box below lists several strategies that were first discussed by Tarone (1981):

I. Paraphrase:
A. Approximation: use of a single target language vocabulary item or structure, which the learner knows is not correct, but which shares enough semantic features in common with the desired item to satisfy the speaker (e.g., pipe for waterpipe)
B. Word coinage: the learner makes up a new word in order to communicate a desired concept (e.g., airball for balloon)
C. Circumlocution: the learner describes the characteristics or elements of the object or action instead of using the appropriate target language item or structure ("She is, uh, smoking something. I don't know what's its name. That's, uh, Persian, and we use in Turkey, a lot of.")

II. Borrowing:
A. Literal translation: the learner translates word for word from the native language (e.g., "He invites him to drink," for "They toast one another.")
B. Language switch: the learner uses the native language term without bothering to translate (e.g., balon for balloon, tirtil for caterpillar)

III. Appeal for assistance: the learner asks for the correct term (e.g., "What is this? What called?")

IV. Mime: the learner uses nonverbal strategies in place of a lexical item or action (e.g., clapping one's hands to illustrate applause)

V. Avoidance:
A. Topic avoidance: the learner simply tries not to talk about concepts for which the target language item or structure is not known
B. Message abandonment: the learner begins to talk about a concept but is unable to continue and stops in mid-utterance

(Adapted from Tarone, 1981, pp. 286–287)

Identify the communication strategies used in the following examples. Imagine that these utterances were made by hotel guests calling the front desk clerk for assistance. Underline each instance of a strategy from Tarone's list and label it using her terms. (Hint: There may be more than one communication strategy in some of the texts below.)

Text 1

"It is, uh, the thing that make the hair hot. You know, when you clean the hair and then after—that thing that make the hair hot when the hair has water. It's, uh, it use electric to make the hair hot. Is not in the room and I want to use it."

Text 2

"So, uh, now, my hair is wet. And I must go to the party. So now, I need that machine, that little machine. What is the name? How do you call it in English?"

Text 3

"We say in Spanish *secadora*—the dryer, but is for the hair. The dryer of the hair. Do you have a dryer of the hair? I need one please."

Text 4

(Imagine that this guest is at the hotel's front desk talking directly to the clerk.) "Yes, uhm, please, I need, you know the thing, I do this" [gestures brushing her hair and blow-drying it] "after I am washing my hair. Do you have this thing?"

Accuracy-oriented approaches, such as the Grammar-translation and Audiolingual Methods, would view utterances like those in the Action box above as problems. But when the teaching focus emphasizes communication, these strategies are seen as ways of continuing a conversation and conveying meaning.

6. Assessing speaking

A major concern for teachers is how we can assess students' speaking abilities in the new language. In some regards, testing speaking is not as straightforward as testing grammar or vocabulary. In this part of the chapter, we will consider three approaches to assessing speaking, as well as different procedures for scoring speaking tests. We will begin by discussing the four basic criteria to keep in mind as we devise, use, or adapt tests of speaking and pronunciation.

First, we want to make sure that we are testing what we are teaching and what the students want to be learning. Doing so is fair and appropriate. A test that measures what it is intended to measure is called a "valid" test. There are many different kinds of **validity**, but the central concept is that we determine in advance what we want to measure. We then design items, tasks, or prompts for the test that measure that construct.

Second, we want to be sure that a test or an assessment procedure is reliable. **Reliability** is concerned with consistency. For instance, if you tape record your students speaking in English and ask another teacher to evaluate the students' speech using a ten-point scale, you would be unhappy if your colleague ran out of time and rushed through the last several recordings, or if that teacher got tired and grumpy about the work and was more severe with the last recordings as a result. The resulting change in the teacher's ratings is an example of unreliability. Specifically, it is a problem in "rater reliability" and it is an issue that we must work to avoid or overcome when we evaluate students' speaking skills.

The third criterion is one which teachers understand quite well—**practicality**. This term refers to the fact that a test or other assessment procedure can only be useful if it does not make unreasonable demands on resources, including time, money, and personnel. Interviewing each student for thirty minutes might be a very thorough way to assess his or her speaking skills, but if you are teaching several classes a day, and especially if they are large classes, then interviewing all your students for thirty minutes apiece would be very impractical.

The fourth criterion is **washback** (or **instructional impact**). This concept is often defined as the effect a test has on teaching and learning. (See Cheng, Watanabe, and Curtis, 2004, for more information.) Does the test encourage people to prepare for speaking tasks, or does it cause them to study grammar rules or obscure vocabulary items? I am not suggesting that vocabulary and grammar are unimportant. In fact, developing vocabulary and increasing their confidence in applying grammar rules are appropriate and significant ways for learners to improve their speaking ability if those grammar rules and vocabulary items are practiced in spoken discourse. Washback can be either positive or negative, depending on whether it promotes the development of the skills or knowledge to be learned (positive washback) or hinders that development (negative washback).

Think about the following questions:

What is validity and how does it differ from reliability?
Why is practicality an important issue in assessing learners' speaking skills?
What are positive and negative washback?

Think about an important test that you have taken. (It can be any test, but a speaking test would be ideal.) How did you prepare for that test? If you were taking a language class at the time, what did your teacher do to help the students prepare for the test? In other words, did it have a positive or negative impact in your case?

Another important issue has to do with whether your approach to testing speaking is direct, indirect, or semi-direct (Clark, 1979). What do these terms mean?

A **direct test** of speaking involves a procedure in which the learners actually speak the target language, interacting with the test administrator or with other students and generating novel utterances. So for instance, an oral proficiency interview, a conversation, or an unscripted role-play can be considered direct tests of speaking.

An **indirect test** of speaking, on the other hand, is one in which the test-takers do not speak. For example, the students may be given a **conversational cloze test** (Hughes, 1981). A cloze test is a written text about a paragraph in length in which words have been deleted (usually every seventh or ninth word) and replaced by blank lines. A conversational **cloze test** is one where the original text is the transcript of an actual conversation. The learners' job is to fill in each blank with a word that would be appropriate in the context of that conversation.

Another example of an indirect test of speaking is the phoneme discrimination task, in which the test-takers hear a single word spoken (for example, "bat") and must select the appropriate picture in the test booklet when faced with a picture of a woman patting a dog, a very fat man, and a boy swinging a baseball bat. These may seem like strange and perhaps even invalid ways to test speaking, but an indirect test of speaking assesses the "enabling skills" that are thought to underlie the speaking skills. For example, since it is often assumed that correct pronunciation requires the ability to distinguish between sounds, that ability is considered a prerequisite to being able to produce those sound contrasts.

Indirect tests of speaking can be very practical and reliable. (It is much easier and more time-efficient to administer a conversational cloze passage to forty students and score the results with a pre-set key than it is to have forty different conversations with students and train raters to evaluate their conversational competence.) However, the students may feel that their speaking skills have not been adequately or fairly assessed (a validity concern). In addition, using indirect procedures may send the message to students that it is not important for them to practice speaking in English since they won't be evaluated on their speaking (an example of negative washback).

What then, are **semi-direct tests** of speaking? This term has been applied in contexts where students actually speak (that is, they produce oral language), but they don't interact in a conversation, interview, or role-play. In other words, the test-takers listen to prompts and tasks delivered by a recorded voice, and also respond by talking to a recording device. Semi-direct tests have the advantage that they are easy to administer to several students at once (e.g., in a classroom or language laboratory), so they are practical. Also, students know they will have to speak during the procedure; so semi-direct tests may generate positive washback. However, many people feel awkward talking to a tape recorder and responding to a disembodied voice from an anonymous person, so there is often an artificial feeling about semi-direct tests of speaking.

There is no absolute right or wrong choice among direct, semi-direct, or indirect tests of speaking. You must choose appropriate assessment procedures after carefully considering your own teaching contexts and the students' needs. The main goal is to devise, use, or adapt valid and reliable tests of speaking that are practical for your situation and which generate positive washback.

Reflection

Think about your experience with the assessment of foreign language speaking skills. Perhaps you recall a test you have taken as a language learner, or one that you have used as a language teacher. Was your speaking ever tested? If so, were the assessment tasks direct, indirect, or semi-direct, or some combination of these approaches? Share your example with a colleague or classmate.

One more important question about assessing learners' speaking skills has to do with how those skills are evaluated. Are they scored or rated? If they are rated, who will do the rating and what criteria will be used to evaluate the students' speech? These are matters of the scoring criteria that are used.

There are three main methods for scoring students' speaking skills: objective scoring, analytic scoring, and holistic scoring (Bailey, 1998). Which approach you use depends in part on what skills or knowledge you are trying to assess and partly on the tasks the learners do. The choice is also influenced by (and influences) the washback message you wish to send to the students.

Objective scoring does not involve any judgment during the scoring process (though a great deal of judgment may be involved in determining the correct answers to compile the key). Truly objective scoring can be done by an untrained person using a scoring key. In many cases, objective scoring can be done by a computer (e.g., in computer-delivered tests or with scannable answer sheets where students mark their answers). Typically there is one and only one correct answer to each objectively scored test item.

In contrast, analytic scoring and holistic scoring both involve some judgment and usually involve training raters to use the assessment system. What then is the difference between these two approaches?

In **holistic ratings**, a speech sample (such as an oral interview, a recorded conversation, or a passage that a learner reads aloud) is given one overall evaluation, which may be a rating (a "six" on a ten-point scale) or a designation (pass versus not pass, or the "advanced" designation in a system that consists of novice, intermediate, advanced, or superior categories).

Analytic ratings, on the other hand, involve rating systems in which the abilities underlying the speaking skill have been analyzed (hence the name, *analytic*) and the test-takers are evaluated on how well they perform the various sub-skills. For example, some people have used analytic scales that include the categories of vocabulary, grammar, pronunciation, and fluency in evaluating speaking. Others include the categories of appropriateness and the ability to execute certain speech acts effectively. The analytic categories that you include in your rating system amount to your theory of what speaking is.

Action

Think about the students you teach or plan to teach. What would be the appropriate categories to include in an analytic rating scale to assess their English speaking skills? Make a list of the categories you would use. Share your list with a few classmates or colleagues to get their opinions.

7. Conclusion

The goal of this chapter has been to examine the concept of speaking and to introduce a number of factors to consider when we are deciding how it can be taught. The first part of the chapter defined speaking and presented a model of spoken language that shows how many components come into play when we are speaking. We looked at the components of communicative competence and read about three main methods for teaching languages, focusing on how speaking is taught in each. Finally, we considered some issues related to the assessment of speaking and pronunciation. These ideas will be explored in more depth in the next three chapters.

 Further readings

Bygate, M. 1987. *Speaking.* Oxford: Oxford University Press.

This book is based on reasonable and realistic tasks for future teachers to do. It has a very helpful chapter on learner strategies of communication.

Pridham, F. 2000. *The Language of Conversation.* London: Routledge.

This is an excellent book written in non-technical language. It explains the regular systems underlying conversations in English. I recommend it highly.

van Lier, L. 1995. *Introducing Language Awareness.* London: Penguin English.

This little book was written for the general public. It explains a great deal of the linguistic background information this chapter focuses on in an entertaining way, with many examples and helpful figures.

 Helpful Web site

Speech, Pronunciation, & Listening Interest Section (www.soundsofenglish.org/SPLIS/)

This is the official site of the Speech, Pronunciation, & Listening Interest Section (SPLIS) of the international TESOL association. In addition to information about the interest section, the site includes discussions of pronunciation issues and information about teaching pronunciation. There are also links to relevant Websites, as well as resource books, pronunciation activities, articles, and an "ask the experts" section.

References

Asher, J. J., J.A. Kusoda, and R. de la Torre. 1993. Learning a Second Language Through Commands: The Second Field Test. In J.W. Oller, Jr. (ed.), *Methods that Work: Ideas for Literacy and Language Teachers* (3rd ed.). Boston, MA: Heinle & Heinle, 3–21.

Bachman, L. 1990. *Fundamentals of Language Testing*. Oxford: Oxford University Press.

Bailey, K.M. 1998. *Learning About Language Assessment: Dilemmas, Decisions and Directions*. Boston, MA: Heinle & Heinle.

Bygate, M. 2001. *Speaking*. Oxford: Oxford University Press.

Canale, M. and M. Swain. 1980. Theoretical Bases of Communicative Approaches to Second Language Testing and Teaching. *Applied Linguistics*, 1(1): 1–47.

Cheng, L., Y. Watanabe, and A. Curtis. 2004. *Washback in Language Testing: Research Contexts and Methods*. Mahwah, NJ: Lawrence Erlbaum.

Clark, J.L.D. 1979. Direct and Semi-direct Tests of Speaking Ability. In E. J. Briere & F. B. Hinofotis (eds.), *Concepts in Language Testing*. Washington, DC: TESOL, 35–49.

Douglas, D. 2000. *Assessing Languages for Specific Purposes*. Cambridge: Cambridge University Press.

Ellis, R. 1990. *Instructed Second Language Acquisition: Learning in the Classroom*. Oxford: Basil Blackwell.

Florez, M.A.C. 1999. *Improving Adult English Language Learners' Speaking Skills*. ERIC Digest ED435204. Retrieved July 7, 2002 from ERIC database.

Gass, S.M. 1997. *Input, Interaction, and the Second Language Learner*. Mahwah, NJ: Lawrence Erlbaum Associates.

Gumperz, J. J. and D. Tannen. 1979. Individual and Social Differences in Language Use. In W. Wang and C. Fillmore (eds.), *Individual Differences in Language Ability and Language Behavior*. New York, NY: Academic Press, 305–325.

Hammerly, H. 1991. *Fluency and Accuracy: Toward Balance in Language Teaching and Learning*. Clevedon: Multilingual Matters, Ltd.

Hughes, D. 1981. Conversational Cloze as a Measure of Oral Ability. *ELT Journal*, 35(2): 161–168.

Larsen-Freeman, D. and M.H. Long. 1991. *An Introduction to Second Language Acquisition Research*. London: Longman.

Lazaraton, A. 2001. Teaching Oral Skills. In M. Celce-Murcia (ed.), *Teaching English as a Second or Foreign Language* (3rd ed.). Boston, MA: Heinle & Heinle, 103–115.

Nunan, D. 2003. Methodology. In D. Nunan (ed.), *Practical English Language Teaching*. New York, NY: McGraw-Hill ESL/ELT, 3–22.

Richards, J., J. Platt, and H. Weber. 1985. *Longman Dictionary of Applied Linguistics*. London: Longman.

Richards, J.C. and T.S. Rodgers. 1986. *Approaches and Methods in Language Teaching: A Description and Analysis*. Cambridge: Cambridge University Press.

Savignon, S.J. 1991. Communicative Language Teaching: The State of the Art. *TESOL Quarterly,* 25(2): 261–277.

Tarone, E. 1981. Some Thoughts on the Notion of Communication Strategy. *TESOL Quarterly,* 15(3): 285–295.

van Lier, L. 1995. *Introducing Language Awareness*. London: Penguin English.

Chapter **Two**

Speaking for beginning level learners

At the end of this chapter, you should be able to:

 describe how speaking is typically taught to beginning level learners.

 explain the following key principles for supporting the teaching of speaking to beginning level students: provide something to talk about; create opportunities for learners to interact by using groupwork and pairwork; and manipulate the physical arrangements to promote speaking practice.

 identify several important communication strategies for supporting the teaching of speaking to beginning students.

 create materials and activities based on the following task and activity types: conversations and interviews; information gaps and jigsaw activities; controlled conversations; scripted dialogues, drama, and role-plays; logic puzzles; picture-based speaking activities; and physical actions.

 examine pieces of classroom interaction and identify the principles underpinning the instructional sequences.

 explain four different purposes for assessment: placement tests, diagnostic tests, progress tests, and achievement tests.

 use a classroom introduction activity as a speaking diagnostic test.

1. Introduction

The *Practical English Language Teaching* series as a whole uses learners' level of proficiency as a basic organizing principle. In this chapter, we will look at the teaching of speaking to beginning level students. In Chapter 3, we will focus on intermediate students, and in Chapter 4, we will look at advanced learners. Finally, in Chapter 5 we will consider key issues in teaching speaking regardless of the levels.

The categories of beginning, intermediate, and advanced learners are actually rather loose and cover a wide range of ability. In fact, some language programs and some textbook series use five or six classifications: true beginner, high (or "false") beginner, lower intermediate, intermediate, upper intermediate, and advanced. However, you should know that these terms may be used somewhat differently from one region to another, and even from one program to another.

In Section 2 of this chapter, we will first consider some **syllabus** design issues in teaching speaking to beginning learners and **false beginners** (that is, learners who have had some formal instruction but who can't really use the language productively to express their own ideas). We will then look at some principles for teaching speaking to beginning students in Section 3 before turning to Section 4, "Tasks and materials," which provides examples of materials and describes activities that can be used with beginning students. Pronunciation issues are the topic for Section 5 and "Speaking in the classroom" is the focus of Section 6. Finally, "Assessing beginning learners" will be the topic of Section 7.

What does it mean to be a "beginning" or a "lower-level" language learner? According to the American Council on the Teaching of Foreign Languages (ACTFL), beginning level students can be characterized as follows:

- Oral production consists of isolated words and learned phrases within very predictable areas of need.
- Vocabulary is sufficient only for handling simple, elementary needs and expressing basic courtesies.
- Utterances rarely consist of more than two or three words and show frequent long pauses and repetition of interlocutor's words.
- Speaker may have some difficulty producing even the simplest utterances.

The ACTFL guidelines also say that at this level some speakers will be understood only with great difficulty. Given these limitations, what can teachers do to help beginning students develop their English speaking skills?

Talk to three beginning level learners or false beginners of English. According to these students, what are their main goals for studying English? What are their current strengths? What areas do they most want to improve upon first? Now think about your own assessment of these people's speaking skills? What do you think are their current strengths in speaking English? What areas should they work to improve first? Fill out the chart below:

Which person	His/Her ideas	Your ideas
Learner #1		
Learner #2		
Learner #3		

Where your ideas differ from those of the individual learners, what accounts for the differences?

2. Syllabus design issues

There are many differences in teaching English as a foreign or second language. When we teach a language in the country where it is spoken (such as English in Australia, Canada, New Zealand, the U.K. or the U.S.) it is called **English as a Second Language (ESL)**. In contexts where English is not the prevalent language used for communicating (such as Argentina, Oman, Kazakhstan, or Thailand), we talk about teaching **English as a Foreign Language (EFL)**. Another way to discuss this difference is to contrast "English as a local language" and "English as a remote language" (Hammerly, 1991, p. 148). There are important practical concerns to remember in teaching speaking to learners in these two contexts (Bailey, 2003).

Reflection

Think about the differences between EFL and ESL contexts for learners of English. What would be some contrasts in listening—that is, in the opportunities for hearing English in EFL and ESL settings? What might be the different expectations for learners to speak English in EFL and ESL situations?

If you are teaching EFL (or plan to teach) in your home culture, you are probably already aware of the challenges that learners face when their exposure to English outside the classroom is limited. But if you come from a country where English is the dominant language (or is widely available outside English classrooms), you may need to develop skills and strategies for helping your EFL students gain access to the target language. Many of the ideas in this book are intended to help you create and increase opportunities for your students in EFL situations to speak English.

Likewise, if you are teaching EFL, you will need to be particularly creative in designing a syllabus and planning lessons that promote speaking skills. For beginning learners or false beginners in an EFL context, it can be difficult to find opportunities to listen to and speak English. In these situations, the classroom is extraordinarily important in providing input and practice opportunities for the learners. Classroom lessons can become safe havens where low-level learners can make mistakes and take risks in a supportive environment with a helpful teacher and classmates who are at approximately the same proficiency level and who may have similar concerns.

In ESL contexts, beginning learners and false beginners can get ample input (that is, a great deal of English is available to be heard and read), but they can also get discouraged by the need to communicate in English, and by people's expectations that they will be able to do so. In ESL situations then, lessons can help learners prepare for the kinds of tasks they must be able to do in English outside the classroom.

Syllabus design issues are related to decisions about what to teach in any given course. When teaching speaking to low-level students, it is important not to overwhelm them with unreasonable expectations for oral production. At the same time, we shouldn't underestimate what they can do given the right guidance.

The ACTFL guidelines describing novice speakers of a language refer to the use of "learned phrases." These phrases are also sometimes called "fixed expressions" or "formulaic expressions" because they follow a fixed formula and do not change depending on the speech circumstances. In contrast, English verbs must be conjugated for person (*I speak, you speak,* but *he, she* or *it speaks*) and nouns must be marked for plurality *(one shoe, two shoes; one child, two children)* or possession *(John's hat, the students' books).* Formulaic expressions are useful and efficient because the learner doesn't have to change them. Nunan (2005, p. 173) defines a **formula** as "a piece of language that learners memorize as a single functional 'chunk' without... breaking it down into its different grammatical elements." Some useful formulaic expressions for beginning learners include, "I dunno," "A little more slowly please," and "How do you say...?" (Be careful though! A British friend tells me that "I dunno" might be considered rude in England or Canada.)

Make a list of at least five more formulaic expressions that would be useful for beginning learners of English to know. Compare your list with that of a colleague or classmate. You could combine your lists as the basis for a students' worksheet.

Learning some key formulaic expressions can be very helpful for beginning learners for at least three reasons. First, using expressions such as "How do you spell that?" when encountering a new vocabulary word in a conversation can help learners understand the ongoing interaction, and may actually help them learn the new word. (Asking how a word is spelled can slow the conversation a bit and the spelling may help learners recognize words that they've read before.) Second, using such expressions can help sustain the interaction. That is, native speakers or proficient non-native speakers may be encouraged to continue communicating with beginning speakers who are apparently trying to communicate. Third, formulaic expressions may provide input for the language acquisition process. What does this mean?

Another term for "formulaic expressions" is "unanalyzed chunks"–by which we mean that the learners acquire the expression as a whole without analyzing its component parts. The formula "I dunno" is a good example. A learner who acquires this phrase may see that people use it when they lack information or knowledge. It may be some time before the learner realizes that "dunno" is a phonologically-reduced form of "don't know," and later still before "don't" is recognized as the contracted form of "do not." In other words, when the learner is ready, he can analyze the "unanalyzed chunk" and learn more about how the language works.

A word of caution is needed here. The apt use of formulaic expressions can make beginning learners appear more fluent than they actually are, which can lead to their interlocutors having unrealistically high expectations of them. As a student of beginning French, I loved the formulaic phrase, "Nous avons besoin de…" (we have need of) because it could be followed by any noun to make a request. You can imagine my embarrassment in a restaurant in Los Angeles when the linguist I was with asked how my French class was going, and I told him that day we had learned "Nous avons besoin d'une bouteille de vin"–at which point a nearby waiter handed me the wine list and began speaking rapid-fire idiomatic French to me. Likewise, while traveling in Japan, I have often used the Japanese equivalent of "Excuse me, I don't speak Japanese. Am I in the right place?" (pointing to my ticket in a train station). Unfortunately, the declaration that I don't speak Japanese (which is, sadly, quite true) is often over-ridden in my listeners' minds by the memorized chunks of Japanese language I am using, and about half the time people respond to my question in Japanese!

The types of syllabus designs used around the world are quite varied, and speaking is taught and practiced in many different curricular contexts. One common format for teaching speaking is the conversation class. This offering is very popular in language schools. It typically means that learners engage in loosely structured conversations with a teacher. It seldom means that teachers and learners actively investigate the structure of English conversations, or analyze how to participate successfully in them.

Speaking is also taught in combination with other skills, most typically listening. Or there will be separate speaking classes in the broader curriculum of intensive English programs, in which students use the vocabulary and grammar structures they have studied in other classes.

Another curricular offering is the public speaking course, in which the syllabus goes beyond conversational interaction and helps learners prepare to speak to audiences. Such courses are more common at the intermediate and advanced levels than they are with beginning students.

Some syllabuses revolve around textbooks. In the following excerpt from a table of contents, the chapter titles are based on topics for discussion (reflecting the principle that people need something to talk about–see page 36). The speaking tasks are based partly on topics (such as "talking about transportation") and partly on speech acts (see page 5). The pronunciation activities in the beginning level textbook focus on phonological processes (such as reductions) or linguistic categories (e.g., word families). Others are based on typical trouble spots, such as pronouncing "teens and tens."

Example 1

1. **Neighborhoods, Cities, and Towns**
   a. **Speaking tasks:** talking about days and dates, saying dates, talking about transportation, role-playing personal information
   b. **Pronunciation:** contractions

2. **Shopping and e-commerce**
   a. **Speaking tasks:** comparing prices and stores, identifying clothes, describing clothes, interviewing peers about shopping habits, role-playing returns to a store
   b. **Pronunciation:** reductions

3. **Friends and Family**
   a. **Speaking tasks:** discussing appearance, leaving voicemail messages, describing people, interviewing peers about keeping in touch with friends and family, interviewing peers about conversation topics, role-playing greetings
   b. **Pronunciation:** reductions

4. **Health Care**
   a. **Speaking tasks:** discussing complaints, discussing health advice and habits, talking about body parts, role-playing problems and advice, discussing exercise
   b. **Pronunciation:** reductions

5. **Men and Women**
   a. **Speaking tasks:** discussing dating etiquette, discussing invitations, discussing celebrations
   b. **Pronunciation:** reductions

6. **Sleep and Dreams**
   a. **Speaking tasks:** interviewing peers about sleep and dreams, role-playing disagreement, discussing a lecture, telling your dreams
   b. **Pronunciation:** teens and tens

7. **Work and Lifestyles**
   a. **Speaking tasks:** interviewing peers about jobs, talking about future plans, interviewing peers about the future
   b. **Pronunciation:** majors vs. job titles

8. **Food and Nutrition**
   a. **Speaking tasks:** discussing nutrition and food, role-playing ordering in a restaurant, talking about recipes, presenting a recipe, discussing nutritional contents of food, comparing food labels
   b. **Pronunciation:** reductions

9. **Great Destinations**
   a. **Speaking tasks:** describing vacation destinations, asking about and discussing flight information, getting trip information from a travel agency, talking about sports
   b. **Pronunciation:** word families

10. **Our Planet**
   a. **Speaking tasks:** discussing environmental messages, discussing reasons for species being endangered, researching endangered species, debating cnvironmental goals
   b. **Pronunciation:** emphasis

Adapted from Thrush, Blass and Baldwin, 2002, pp. viii-ix

You may have noticed that many of the pronunciation topics in this table of contents are related to **reductions**–phonological processes in which sounds are lost or muffled (e.g., when *little* is pronounced as "lil"). Such reductions are very common in spoken English.

Action

Review the table of contents in Example 1. Choose a chapter that sounds interesting to you. With a friend, brainstorm some speaking activities you could try in class if you were using this textbook with a group of beginner or false beginner students.

There are many different ways to organize a syllabus, and commercially produced textbooks may or may not fit the needs and goals of the learners you are working with. Often you will need to supplement the text with creative speaking activities of your own.

3. Principles for teaching speaking to beginning learners

In this section we will consider three principles which can influence and inform our decisions as we teach speaking to beginning and false beginning learners. These principles are:

- Provide something for learners to talk about.
- Create opportunities for students to interact by using groupwork or pairwork.
- Manipulate physical arrangements to promote speaking practice.

We will discuss each of these principles in turn, and highlight some of their practical implications for teaching speaking to beginning students and false beginners.

1. Provide something for learners to talk about.

As we noted in our look at Example 1 (pp. 34–35), when people choose to speak, it is usually about *something*. They want something, or they find a topic or incident interesting and want to comment on it. They wish to share ideas or emotions. There is usually some communicative need that moves people to talk. As Pennington (1995, p. x) puts it, teachers should attend to the communicative needs and purposes of language learners. Sometimes in language classrooms, teachers seem to forget the natural joy and enthusiasm of talking about something interesting, or accomplishing a genuine purpose for communicating with others.

I remember seemingly endless substitution drills in my audio-lingual French class, with the students repeating the teacher's sentence about the pen of my aunt being on the table. Then the teacher would cue another noun

("Hat!") and suddenly we were all chanting in chorus about the hat of my aunt being on the table, and so on through a list of every mundane possession one's aunt might possibly have. The idea of a substitution drill, of course, is that the learners would form habits through this practice, and the structure in question would become automatic. As a result, supposedly the language learner could quickly and effortlessly use the pattern, "The (noun) of my (noun) is on the (noun)." In fact, another name for "substitution drills" is "pattern practice."

When the students in the French class had mastered many common nouns, the syllabus dictated prepositions, and we were soon chanting variations on "The (noun) of my (noun) is IN the (noun)" and "The (noun) of my (noun) is UNDER the (noun)"–but who cared? All this practice and repetition was so unreal, so unmotivated, so boring! I don't recall learning a single thing about any of my classmates or their ideas, aspirations, or goals for learning French.

People talk to communicate–that is, to express themselves, to get goods and services, to influence people, to convey meanings and messages, and to enjoy the company of others. Admittedly, these are challenging goals when one is at the beginning or false beginner levels of language learning, but the point still holds: People need to talk about something, and ideally that should be something of interest to them.

Thus, one key principle in teaching speaking is that teachers should provide something for learners to talk about. This doesn't mean that only teachers can nominate topics–not at all! Teachers should be open to those topics that the learners want to talk about, and incorporate them into lessons whenever possible. (See the discussion of personalization as a principle on page 97 of Chapter 3.) But it does mean that you should go into your speaking lessons prepared with interesting topics or ideas to stimulate conversations and discussions.

Reflection

Think about a beginning language class you have taken. What were the sorts of topics you talked about in class? Were the discussions enjoyable? Memorable? Did you enjoy discussing some topics more than others, or speaking with some of your classmates more than others?

In speaking lessons, pictures and "manipulables" can provide the motivation for talking. **Manipulables** is just a fancy word for things you can handle, move or manipulate in some way. For example, you can buy Cuisenaire Rods™ or Legos™ and use them as the basis of many communicative activities. (Cuisenaire Rods are brightly colored wooden rods of varying lengths, from about three inches to one-quarter inch long. Legos are small plastic building blocks that snap together to form structural designs.) But you can also use other things that are cheap or even free, or you can ask students to bring such things to class. Decks of playing cards, pieces from board games, the four smallest denomination coins in a country's currency and even bits of colored paper (a red square, a blue circle, a yellow triangle, a green rectangle) can be the basis of many interesting speaking activities in language classrooms. If you are working in a school without many resources, consider using different kinds or sizes of leaves, shells, stones or seedpods, or different lengths of sticks.

Using pictures as the basis of speaking lessons also gives the learners something to talk about, something to focus on other than their own uncertainty with the new language. Whether you use colored photographs from calendars, advertisements cut from magazines, or pictures you locate on the Internet, photographs add interest to speaking lessons and can motivate people to speak. In Section 4 of this chapter, we will consider some picture-based activities to use in speaking lessons.

2. Create opportunities for students to interact by using groupwork or pairwork.

Sometimes students–perhaps especially those at the lower levels–can be anxious about speaking out in class. One way to overcome their reticence and increase their opportunities to speak is to use pairwork and groupwork. According to Pennington (1995, p. x), using pairwork and groupwork can improve learners' motivation and promote choice, independence, creativity, and realism. Pairwork and groupwork also provide feedback to the learner from sources other than the teacher (i.e., from their peers).

Pairwork and groupwork are configurations of people for doing activities, rather than activity types per se. **Pairwork**, as the name suggests, involves two students working together to complete a task or exercise using the target language. **Groupwork** is three or more students working together. In my experience, three students per group is ideal, because three students cannot generate more than one conversation, as four students can, so with three students per group it is easier to keep them focused on the task at hand.

Pairwork and groupwork have been widely used by teachers in **Communicative Language Teaching (CLT)**. In the early days of CLT, research showed that students working in pairs get more individual talking time than students working in teacher-fronted classes. Early classroom research revealed that students talking in pairs also perform a wider range of speech acts, including those normally performed by teachers (Long, Adams, McLean, and Castaños, 1976).

Sometimes novice teachers worry about the chaos that can occur if they relinquish the floor to the students during a speaking activity It's true that groupwork and pairwork can be noisy, but if the learners are on task, it's a great kind of noise that ensues! Here are some tips for making sure that you can control the activity to the extent that you feel comfortable:

1. Set the task clearly first. Either provide written instructions on slips of paper for the students or post them on the chalkboard or overhead transparency.
2. Start with pair interactions, and then when the students are used to pairing up quickly and quietly, move to groups of three, and then later use larger groups if you want to.
3. At first give instructions about how to get into groups (e.g., have the students say numbers aloud in order, 1-2-3, 1-2-3, and so on, and then form groups by having three "1's" sit together, and so on).
4. Set specific time limits for how long students will be working in pairs or groups.
5. Give clear guidance as to what is expected at the end of the pairwork or groupwork. For example, you might say, "In five minutes, each group sends one person to the chalkboard to write down your list of favorite foods. All the group members help that person spell the words correctly."

As you gain experience in working with groups and pairs of students, you will develop your own grouping and pairing strategies.

3. Manipulate physical arrangements to promote speaking practice.

It can be difficult to get students to talk with one another in a new language, but that difficulty is often exacerbated by the traditional classroom arrangement of desks facing forward toward the teacher's zone. Changing the physical environment can encourage speaking activities, partly because it partially alters the power structure of the traditional English classroom. Here are some ways to work with the seating and other aspects of the environment to encourage speaking.

The **inside-outside circle** is a technique for giving students the chance to repeat a conversation or interview with several new people, in order to build fluency and confidence. Form two concentric circles of students. The people on the outside face inwards while the people on the inside face outward. Thus, each person is facing a partner. The students interview these partners for two or three minutes to get the answers to preset questions (which you can devise yourself or which you and the students can brainstorm together). After a few minutes, the students change partners, for instance, by the people in the outer circle moving three partners to the right. This step is repeated as often as the activity continues to be useful.

Tango seating is a simple seating arrangement designed to force people to use oral communication during information gap tasks that involve drawing pictures, following maps, or creating designs or structures from verbal descriptions. Picture a couple dancing in the classic Argentine tango style. The woman's left hand is on the man's right shoulder. Her right hand is in his left hand. His right hand is on her back, and they are facing in totally opposite directions. Now picture the couple sitting down in desks facing the opposite directions, with their right shoulders together. They can speak to and hear one another, but neither can see what is on the other person's desk or lap. This is tango seating.

Finally, the **cocktail party technique** is a quick way to get students talking to new partners and to break up the routine of sitting during language lessons. In using the cocktail party technique, the teacher sets a brief speaking task first. Make sure the instructions are simple and clear. (It will help if you write them on the chalkboard or an overhead transparency projected on a screen, so students can consult them as needed.) In this procedure, the learners talk briefly with different people and then move on to talk to someone new, as if they were at a social gathering. After they have completed the task, they sit down again. The physical act of sitting gives you, as the teacher, an easy way to see when the activity is coming to an end.

Action

Think about two or three speaking activities that you would like to try with your own English students. (If you are not yet teaching, think about when you do become a teacher.) Share your list with a classmate or colleague and explain why you selected these particular activities.

In summary, we have examined three key principles to keep in mind when teaching speaking to beginning students and false beginners:

1. Provide something for learners to talk about.
2. Create opportunities for students to interact by using group-work or pairwork.
3. Manipulate the physical environment to promote speaking practice.

In the chapters that follow, we will build on these principles. They are important in working with intermediate and advanced learners, too. Keep in mind, however, that there are additional important principles that have not been addressed here.

4. Tasks and materials

The purpose of this section is to describe and exemplify a range of task and exercise types that can be used to teach speaking to beginning learners. The aim is not to generate an exhaustive list, but rather to offer you sample tasks and exercise types that you can use as models to develop your own materials. The Reflection and Action boxes provide you with opportunities to analyze these activities and develop your own examples. The following exercise types are described and exemplified:

1. Conversations, controlled (or guided) conversations, and interviews
2. Information gap and jigsaw activities
3. Scripted dialogues, drama, and role-playing
4. Logic puzzles
5. Picture-based activities
6. Physical actions in speaking lessons

Regardless of the course focus or level, all speaking activities can be characterized as more or less interactive. A recited monologue is spoken by one person without others contributing to the discourse, whereas a conversation, by definition, is highly interactive. A lecture can be largely non-interactive, but a seminar discussion is more interactive than a lecture. Different kinds of interactions occur in different **speech events** (situated, identifiable, and somewhat predictable genres of spoken language associated with certain contexts). Lectures and seminars are two examples of speech events.

Likewise, the speaking activities in various speech events can involve more or less original language. At its most creative, language is generated entirely by the speakers (as in a spontaneous conversation in which the speakers choose what to say to one another as the discourse continues). In other contexts, language can be largely recited–in rituals, in theatre productions, or in contexts where speakers read aloud what someone else has written. (Of course, students can also recite or read aloud what they themselves have written.)

Activities for teaching and practicing speaking range along a continuum from totally scripted speech, to guided output by the learners, to completely novel, self-directed output. Of course, there is a role for repetition and reading aloud as part of practicing speaking skills and building confidence and automaticity. But it is important to remember that our students are not learning English just so they can repeat after others or read aloud from prepared texts. They also want to be able to carry on conversations, express their feelings, explain their own ideas, and get things done using English. For these reasons, it is crucial for teachers to provide opportunities for students to practice creative uses of the language.

In this section, we will examine several task types. These are basic activity structures that can be adapted for students at any level (and, in fact, for learners of any language). We will revisit some of these tasks and activities in subsequent chapters of the book as we consider the teaching of speaking to learners at more advanced proficiency levels.

Reflection

Think about a time when you were taking a language course. What were some of the activities your teachers had you do in class to practice speaking? What about activities that were used to learn and to practice the correct pronunciation of the target language? Which of these activities were successful and which were not? Are there any patterns in terms of those that you found to be helpful and those you thought were not so helpful?

1. Conversations and interviews

Conversation is one of the most basic and pervasive forms of human interaction. But carrying on a conversation in the target language can be very difficult for beginning students and false beginners, for many reasons. For example, carrying on a conversation in English involves selecting vocabulary, applying the grammar rules, pronouncing the English sounds, and understanding the other person. Doing all these things at once is quite demanding.

A **guided conversation** (also called **controlled conversation**) is an old technique from the audiolingual era that is still useful for lower-level students. In a guided conversation, "the students are given a framework within which to build their sentences, but the actual choice of what they will say is left up to them" (Allen and Valette, 1977, p. 231). Here is an example of a guided conversation using a one-sided script:

I: Robert, why such a sad face?

You: _____

I: Where did you lose it?

You: _____

I: What is it worth?

You: _____

I: Why didn't you buy another one?

You: _____

I: To whom are you going to tell what happened, your mother or your father?

You: _____

I: Why?

You: _____

I: Will your parents give you the money you need?

You: _____

I: Well, what are you going to do?

You: _____

Adapted from Allen and Valette, 1977, p. 233

Action

Write a one-sided conversation using the example above. Try it out with a classmate or colleague.

True conversations are unscripted, free-ranging discourses involving two or more people. In a conversation the topic can change and the individuals take turns, which are **contingent** (that is, the utterances build on the different speakers' contributions). By definition, conversations are interactive: Although one speaker is sometimes more talkative than another, in a conversation, two or more individuals communicate.

Some textbooks just give topics for conversations, but others deal specifically with HOW to participate in conversations. An important part of carrying on a conversation is to use communication strategies to prevent or repair communication breakdowns. In Chapter 1 (see pp. 19–20), we considered several communication strategies. For beginning learners and false beginners in particular, it is very important to have some strategies for getting help when they don't understand what someone says. Here is some advice for learners about how to ask for clarification and confirm their understanding:

Example 3

Asking for repetition
1. Could you repeat that, please?

2. Would you mind repeating that, please?

3. I'm sorry, I didn't catch that.

4. _____

5. _____

Asking for explanation
1. I don't understand what you mean by (rehearse). Could you explain that?

2. I'm still not sure what you mean. Would you mind explaining that again?

3. I'm afraid I don't understand. Do you think you could explain that?

4. _____

Springboard to Success: Communication Strategies for the Classroom and Beyond (Skillman and MacMahill, 1996, pp. 30-31)

It is important for teachers to create tasks that encourage learners to speak English. Two ways to get learners to talk to people in English are contact assignments and interviews.

Contact assignments are a type of short, focused interview. These are tasks in which the language learners are obliged to have contact with speakers of the target language. For example, in a second language environment, an information scavenger hunt is a useful activity for getting new students acquainted with the school, the town, or the university campus. A **scavenger hunt** is a kind of party game in which teams of people compete to see who can collect a specified assortment of odd items most quickly—usually by asking neighbors for them. For instance, a scavenger hunt list might include a red button, a cancelled air mail stamp, a newspaper that is at least three days old, a piece of chocolate candy, and so on. None of these items is valuable; the fun is in asking strangers for peculiar items. As a language practice activity, in an information scavenger hunt, teams of two or three students each can be sent out to gather specific information that they cannot get simply by reading signs or menus.

A specific kind of contact assignment is to have students interview people in English. **Interviews** are semi-structured sequences of questions intended to elicit particular information from the people answering the questions. Typically one person takes the role of the interviewer and the other person answers the questions. However, with low-level students it can also be worthwhile to have them conduct the interviews in pairs. That way they can build their confidence and help each other. If the students are at the intermediate proficiency level or lower, it is important to help them brainstorm and practice the questions before they actually interview people. Finally, with beginning students, it is best to have them start by interviewing people they know, rather than talking to strangers in English.

Interviews are conducted to get specific information or to learn about someone's opinions. Conducting an interview in a second or foreign language can be very challenging—especially for low-level learners. However, with support, beginning students and false beginners can be very successful in carrying out interviews, and can practice their English, use communications strategies, and gain confidence in the process. Example 4 provides some guidance about conducting interviews from a textbook for high beginning students:

Example 4

Interviewing

Sometimes you'll need to interview people. In an interview, you generally ask a person a number of questions about one topic. (In a survey, you generally ask many people the same question.)

To begin an interview, you can say the following:

- Excuse me. Could I ask you a few questions for a class?
- Hi. I'm doing a project for my English class. May I ask you a few questions?
- Hello. My name's _____. May I ask you a few short questions for a project in my English class?

During the interview, do the following:

- Listen to the answers.
- Show interest. (Say "Oh?" "Really?" "That's interesting.")
- Take notes. (Remember to bring a pen and paper.)
- Don't be shy. If you don't understand something, ask the person to repeat.

To end the interview, you can say the following:

- Well, thanks a lot.
- Thank you for your time.
- Thanks for your help.

Quest: Listening and Speaking in the Academic World, Book One
(Hartmann and Blass, 2000, pp. 52-53)

2. Information gap and jigsaw activities for beginning level students

The idea of the **information gap** as an organizing concept for a speaking activity is that one person has information that another lacks. They must use English to share that information in order to accomplish a task.

A natural information gap activity for lower-level courses is for one student to tell another about his family. In the process, the listening student must draw a family tree and label the people in that tree with the appropriate names. If your students are also learning to write in English, they can write information about each person as well (e.g., occupations, hobbies, likes and dislikes, and so on). When the speaker has finished describing his family, the listener shows him the family tree and together they sort out any misunderstandings that may have occurred. To make the activity more interactive, the listening student can ask for repetition, clarification, and expansion. The speaker should not look at his partner's work while the drawing is in progress, so be sure to use tango seating (p. 40) or some other way of blocking the speaker's view of the drawing. Here is an example from a textbook that uses the family as a topic of conversation:

Example 5

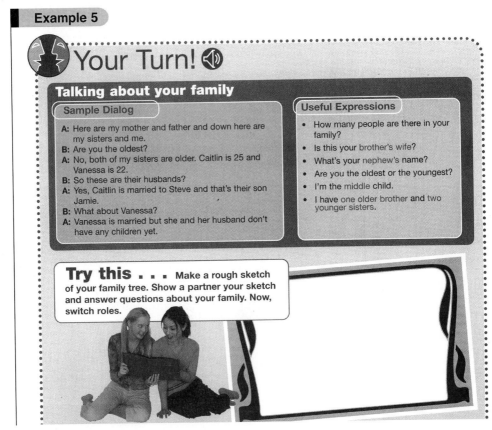

Your Turn!

Talking about your family

Sample Dialog

A: Here are my mother and father and down here are my sisters and me.
B: Are you the oldest?
A: No, both of my sisters are older. Caitlin is 25 and Vanessa is 22.
B: So these are their husbands?
A: Yes, Caitlin is married to Steve and that's their son Jamie.
B: What about Vanessa?
A: Vanessa is married but she and her husband don't have any children yet.

Useful Expressions

- How many people are there in your family?
- Is this your brother's wife?
- What's your nephew's name?
- Are you the oldest or the youngest?
- I'm the middle child.
- I have one older brother and two younger sisters.

Try this . . . Make a rough sketch of your family tree. Show a partner your sketch and answer questions about your family. Now, switch roles.

Listen In, Book 1 (Nunan, 2003, p. 19)

Another natural information gap involves giving directions. For example, one student has the directions to a class party and the other has a map. The first student must give the directions to the second in English. Meanwhile the second student traces the route on the map and asks clarifying questions to make sure he has understood the directions and is marking the map correctly. In this activity it may be helpful if you **pre-teach** some of the vocabulary and typical expressions for giving directions (*turn right, turn left, go straight three blocks, at the corner,* and so on). Here are some useful expressions for asking and giving directions from a textbook designed for beginning and false beginner students:

Example 6

Put It Together

A. Asking for and Giving Directions. `Pair` Use the map on page 31 to ask for and give directions. You can look back at the sample conversations on page 30 and use the expressions in this box.

Go down (or up) one/two/three blocks.*

Turn left/right.   Make a left/right.

Go past the _____.   It's right there.

It's right there on your left/right.   It's across from the _____.

It's on Thorn Drive/Gareth Avenue/Third Street.**

It's next to the _____.

It's on the corner of _____ and _____.

It's in the middle of the block.

* In English, people count *blocks*, not streets.
** Notice that in English, street names don't have *the* before them.

Quest: Listening and Speaking in the Academic World, Book One
(Hartmann and Blass, 2000, p. 35)

My British friend points out that in American English people count blocks rather than streets, so be sure to tell your students that they will encounter some regional variation as they use these expressions.

After students have practiced this activity in class, you can have them give directions over the telephone. The speaking task becomes more challenging under those circumstances, since they can not convey meanings by drawing or gesturing.

Find a map that would be suitable to use in a direction-giving task with your beginning or false-beginner students. (This might be a map of the campus if you are teaching at a university, or a map of the surrounding neighborhood. It can also be the map of a shopping area or a single building if the building is complex enough.) Select several locations on the map that could be used as destinations, so students can give one another the directions for finding a particular site. What sorts of language (vocabulary, grammatical structures, speech acts) will learners need to complete this activity successfully?

Action

Create an information gap activity for student pairs using the map you found. (Each member of the pair must have a copy of the map, but only one member knows the intended destination and he or she is not allowed to say specifically what that is.) Write the procedures for the activity, including specific instructions for the learners to follow. (For instance, you must decide if the listening student may ask clarifying questions, making the task more interactive, or if the listener should remain silent—which puts a greater burden on the direction-giver to be clear and precise.) Try out the activity with a classmate or colleague before using it with a class.

Here are some tips for managing map activities. If your students have not done this kind of task before, it is helpful if you produce a copy of the map on an overhead projector transparency and give the class members individual copies of the map. Before you start the pairwork, do two rounds of the map task with the class as a whole. In the first round, you give the instructions and have the students follow them. Make sure everyone starts from the same place. Give clear and simple directions, pausing to make sure the class members are following the steps you give them. Have the students check with one another during this first round. They should all end up at the intended destination more or less together, even though they were working individually.

For the next round, write several possible destinations on the board. Have one student come to the front and choose a destination behind your back (i.e., so the learners all know the chosen destination but you do not). Then have the class members give *you* directions about how to get from the starting point to the selected place as you trace the route on the overhead projector transparency, thereby giving the class a common visual point of reference as they guide you through the map task.

When it is clear that the students understand the procedure, put them in pairs and give one member of each pair (Student A) an index card with a destination written on it. (You will need to prepare several different destination cards–perhaps ten for a class of thirty students.) When the students are done with this next round of the task, have them pass their destination cards to Student B in the pair sitting to their right (or clockwise). In this way, during the next round, the second member of each pair describes a novel destination to his or her partner.

One more tip: If you are working in a context where photocopying is limited, have the students just trace the routes on the maps with their fingers instead of using pen or pencil. That way you can reuse the photocopied maps again in the future. If you have access to a laminating machine, your maps will last much longer if you can laminate them before you use them in this activity.

Action

Sometimes civic organizations or schools will provide maps for free. Visit a tourist information center in your town or the student center at your school to see if they have appropriate maps that you could use for information gap activities in your class.

When two or more students each have unique information that the others lack, we talk about a "two-way information gap" or "jigsaw activity." This latter term comes from the idea of putting together a jigsaw puzzle, because the various bits of information that the different students have must be combined (using English) to do the task. So, for instance, one student might have a map of San Francisco with routes and schedules for the busses and trolley cars, while another has brochures with the hours and prices of various tourist attractions. The students must pool their information to plan an itinerary that would let them see six different sights in two days. It is the combining and use of two (or more) different sets of information, which gives the activity its jigsaw nature.

3. Scripted dialogues, drama, and role-playing

Different forms of drama can be very useful in teaching speaking classes for language learners. When actors are performing a play, they typically recite lines written by someone else. (Improvisational theatre is an exception to this idea.) The creativity of theatre (in terms of the actors' speaking) lies in how the play is staged and how the actors deliver their lines. Of course, the original playwright's work is highly creative–but here I am using the term "creativity" in the linguistic sense of the speaker generating novel utterances.

As mentioned in Chapter 1, a hallmark of the **Audiolingual Method** was its use of written dialogues, which the students were to memorize and recite. The assumption was that students would eventually have opportunities to use these dialogues in conversation, making appropriate substitutions for the various nouns, adjectives, and verbs in the memorized text. Unfortunately, those dialogues seldom resembled actual conversations, and I remember them as deadly dull.

Beyond the Audiolingual Method, however, there are many uses for scripted texts in teaching speaking. One advantage of using scripts is that the students encounter words and grammar structures in an entertaining and meaningful context. Also, when the speaking text is already written, the learners can focus on the forms they are producing because they don't have to worry about actually generating original language to convey their own meanings.

How can we use a scripted play with beginning or false beginning learners? If you choose a simple but entertaining script with short lines and a plot that is easy to follow, your students may enjoy performing a play and developing their speaking skills in the process. Here is an example of a short play, which I have used with low-level learners. (I'm sorry that I don't know the source of this text. I first saw the play when I was a child and have been using the idea ever since.)

Example 7

A Three-Act Play

Cast of characters:
The Knight
The Villain
The Villain's Servant

The Princess
Two Doors (two students who stand facing each other with their arms outstretched straight in front of them, hands clasped)

(Knocking is heard.)

Villain: Go see who's at the door.

Servant: Yes, master. (Opens the doors.)

Doors: Crrreeak....

Servant: Who are you?

Knight: (Bowing) I am the hero of this story.

Servant: Oh. (He closes the doors.)

Doors: Crrreeak....

Servant: He says he's the hero of this story.

Villain: Curses!! Well, find out what he wants.

Servant: (He opens the doors.)

Doors: Crrreeak....

Servant:	What do you want?
Knight:	I've come to rescue the princess.
Princess:	Oh, my hero! (The knight bows, the princess curtsies.)
Villain:	Curses! Throw him out!
Servant:	(He turns to face the knight.) He says I must throw you out.
Knight:	Ha! Not on your life.
Servant:	*My* life?
Knight:	Out of my way, you fool. (He draws his sword.)
Servant:	(He steps back out of the knight's path.)
Princess:	(She clasps her hands and bats her eyelashes.) Oh, my hero. (The knight bows.)
Villain:	Just what do you think you're doing?
Knight:	I'm rescuing the princess.
Villain:	Over my dead body!
Knight:	Whatever you say. (He lunges at the villain, who steps aside. The knight accidentally stabs the princess.)
Knight:	Oops!
Villain:	You fool!
Servant:	Oh dear!
Princess:	(Dying) My hero….
Doors:	Crrrreeeak….

Of course, there may be some unfamiliar vocabulary here (*curses, to curtsy, to bat one's eyelashes,* and so on). Students can look up new words in the dictionary or guess them from context, especially if you demonstrate the meaning (e.g., when the knight *lunges* at the villain). They can also explain new words to each other or ask you about them as well.

Why is this text called, "A Three-Act Play?" The first time through, you can have the students perform the play at a regular speed, in terms of both their actions and their speech. The play takes about two or three minutes to perform.

The second time, everything is done in slow motion—hand gestures, facial expressions, body movements, and speech. Performing the lines with exaggerated slowness actually gives the students an opportunity to focus on their pronunciation, including the pitch, stress, and intonation contours.

Finally, the third rendition is performed at high speed. Movements are rapid and jerky and the speech is high-pitched and very fast. After practicing a few times at very slow speeds, students find they can speak English very quickly when they do not have to concentrate on what to say. My students have had fun performing this play for their peers and have gained some valuable speaking practice in the process.

A **role-play** is a speaking activity in which the students take the part of other people and interact using the characteristics of those people (for instance, age, gender, occupation, and so on). Or the students can be themselves enacting a novel situation. Often a role-play includes a particular communicative task, such as negotiating a purchase, solving a problem, making a reservation, getting information, and so on. Role-plays can be excellent procedures for helping students learn and practice important speech acts, vocabulary, and grammatical structures.

It is important that you, as the teacher, set up role-plays that are realistic, plausible, and related to the students' needs. For example, while it will be very important for immigrant farm-working parents in California to be able to speak English to officials at their children's school, this situation would not be a realistic role-play for college students in China or Russia. Likewise, being able to give directions in English to tourists would be a realistic need for college students in Hong Kong, but probably not for farm workers in California.

With beginning and false beginning students in particular, you will need to set up role-plays very carefully, to make sure you don't embarrass the learners. After all, using English orally (especially in front of one's peers) can be a risky business! Many learners feel they will appear foolish–especially if they make mistakes. Here are some suggestions to help learners overcome these worries:

1. Make it clear that everyone will do the activity at some point. If there is no way to avoid participation, people will eventually abandon their reluctance.
2. Include time for a planning phase. If students have advanced warning and can think about what they want to say in a role-play, they will be less likely to get very nervous under the pressure of speaking English.
3. Build in a pairwork or groupwork step during the preparation phase, so that learners can interact with and benefit from others in planning their role-play together.
4. Demonstrate the activity the first time you use it so that the students will understand what is expected of them. If you are

teaching in an EFL environment, the students may not have been exposed to role-plays in their previous English classes. If you are teaching in an ESL context, the learners may not have experienced role-plays in education systems of their home countries.

5. Have the students do the role-play in pairs or small groups first before having them do the role-play in front of a larger audience of their classmates.

6. Create a climate in your classroom in general where oral mistakes are seen as natural learning opportunities instead of lapses in judgment or evidence that the students are not motivated.

This last point cannot be over-emphasized: How you as the teacher respond to oral errors will profoundly influence your students' willingness to take risks and speak English in class.

It will also be helpful if you pre-teach a list of useful situation-specific words and phrases the students may need during the role-play. You can even leave them written on the board while the students prepare and do the first rounds of the role-play. This resource will provide the students with some linguistic support as they try to use English in a new situation.

Reflection

In Example 1 on page 34, role-play ideas are provided for all the chapters except 5, 7, 9, and 10. Choose one of these chapters and design a role-play related to the theme of the chapter (for instance, a role-play of a job interview for Chapter 7). Write the instructions for two to four participants. What sort of language (vocabulary, grammatical structures, speech acts) would you expect the learners to need in order to do this role-play successfully? What language would you pre-teach in setting up the role-play task?

Action

Have some students complete the role-play you designed. Record and review the role-play. Did the learners use some of the language you predicted? Given what you learn by listening to the tape, how would you set up the role-play next time?

Remember that your students may need to work up gradually to more demanding speaking tasks. For instance, it makes more sense for students—especially those at the lower levels—to do a role-play about giving directions in English if they have already done a map task about following and giving directions. Those activities will provide students with some practice in giving and taking directions before they have to perform the activity in the interactive context of a role-play.

4. Logic puzzles

Logic puzzles are tasks in which, given a certain number of facts, a person must deduce other facts, typically to complete an information grid. These puzzles are reasoning tasks that can be done by one person, but I have found that they are challenging and stimulating as the basis for groupwork. When they are properly prepared, they make ideal materials for jigsaw activities. We will examine the use of adapted logic puzzles as the basis of speaking activities for beginning students here and for intermediate learners in Chapter 3.

Keep in mind that the clues of logic puzzles provide only limited speaking practice as students read them aloud. The true value of logic puzzles as speaking activities arises in the negotiations the group or pair uses to solve the puzzle. To solve it, students must repeat and review the facts given, restate them, paraphrase to check for understanding, ask questions, and make negative statements (about what is unknown or about what is known <u>not</u> to be the case).

The following logic puzzle (Dell, 2000, p. 5) can be used as the basis of a speaking activity for pairwork or groupwork. The task is for the students to speak English together and figure out the full names of each person as well as what pet each person owns. Before doing this puzzle, it is important that you have a discussion about different cultures' naming conventions. What some cultures consider "last" names are "first" names in other cultures. So you may wish to introduce the concepts of "given names" and "surnames" or "family names."

Clue #1:	Four people all own different pets: Alice, Ms. Black, Ms. Brown, and the fish's owner.
Clue #2:	The cat doesn't belong to Bette.
Clue #3:	The dog doesn't belong to Alice.
Clue #4:	Ms. Grey doesn't own the cat.
Clue #5:	Ms. Grey lives next door to Chloe.
Clue #6:	Bette isn't Ms. Brown.
Clue #7:	Bette doesn't own the fish.
Clue #8:	Ms. Black doesn't own the dog.
Clue #9:	One woman's family name is Ms. Green.
Clue #10:	One woman owns a bird.
Clue #11:	One woman is named Ruth.

Before reading any further, please try to work this logic puzzle, either by yourself or with a classmate or colleague. That way you will have first-hand experience of the thought processes involved. As you work on this, be aware of the many linguistic processes involved in trying to solve the puzzle.

When you are working with a class, you can provide the students with a chart like the one below, or you can have them decide how best to organize the available information themselves. Here's what we know initially by simply tabulating the information from some of the eleven clues above (negative information is given in parentheses):

	Person #1	Person #2	Person #3	Person #4
Given Name	Alice		(not Bette)	(not Bette)
Family Name		Ms. Black	Ms. Brown	
Pet	(not the dog)	(not the dog)		the fish

Up to this point the students will have simply been using English to organize the information given in the most overt clues. But from this point on, they must use logic and discuss their options in filling out the remaining blanks. The answers they would come up with are printed below in a handwriting font. So for example, the first thing they might notice is that if Alice doesn't own the dog, and Ms. Black doesn't own the dog and the unknown person owns the fish, then the dog must belong to Ms. Brown. We also know, from Clue #7, that Bette doesn't own the fish, so now we can deduce that Ms. Black's given name must be Bette. This information has been added to the table below in handwriting font:

Given Name	Alice	Bette	(not Bette)	(not Bette)
Family Name		Ms. Black	Ms. Brown	
Pet	(not the dog)	(not the dog)	the dog	the fish

We can also determine that since neither Alice nor Ms. Bette Black owns the dog or the fish, between them they own the cat and the bird. The students in the group proceed in this manner until they have filled in all the cells in the grid and determined each person's given name, family name, and pet.

Example 8 is an information gap task, based on this logic puzzle. It is designed for two students. Give each pair of students a copy of the blank chart or draw the chart on the chalkboard for them to copy. The clues have simply been divided between the two partners, so that they must use English to share information and solve the puzzle.

Example 8

STUDENT A
Look at the information below. Then share your information with your partner. Together fill in the chart with as much information as you can about the people's names and what kind of pet they each have.

Clue #1:	Four people all own different pets: Alice, Ms. Black, Ms. Brown, and the fish's owner.
Clue #2:	The cat doesn't belong to Bette.
Clue #4:	Ms. Grey doesn't own the cat.
Clue #6:	Bette isn't Ms. Brown.
Clue #8:	Ms. Black doesn't own the dog.
Clue #10:	One woman owns a bird.

STUDENT B
Look at the information below. Then share your information with your partner. Together fill in the chart with as much information as you can about the people's names and what kind of pet they have.

Clue #1:	Four people all own different pets: Alice, Ms. Black, Ms. Brown, and the fish's owner.
Clue #3:	The dog doesn't belong to Alice.
Clue #5:	Ms. Grey lives next door to Chloe.
Clue #7:	Bette doesn't own the fish.
Clue #9:	One woman's family name is Ms. Green.
Clue #11:	One woman is named Ruth.

Adapted from *Dell Logic Puzzles*, 2000, p. 5

Reflection

Predict the sorts of language that students will need to solve the information gap puzzle in Example 8. That is, what sorts of grammatical structures, vocabulary items, and speech acts will students need to use to solve the puzzle? What concepts and vocabulary might you want to pre-teach before having your class of beginning learners or false beginners try this task?

5. Picture-based activities for teaching speaking

Photographs from magazines, calendars, or the Internet can provide learners with many things to talk about. Photos from calendars work particularly well because they are often produced in a large format. Also if the calendars are sealed in cellophane for sale, the back of the calendar typically has a small version of the picture for each month. You can save these small versions of the photos and mount them on index cards or some other stiff paper for use in classroom activities.

There are many reasons for using pictures in language lessons. Here are ten (adapted from Curtis and Bailey, 2001):

1. Pictures provide something to talk about. They can take the focus *off* the language learner and put it on the picture being discussed.
2. Pictures can introduce and illustrate topics of interest to the class which are not dealt with in the textbook, as well as topics beyond the teacher's own expertise (e.g., engineering problems, computer technology, soccer, agriculture).
3. Pictures provide visual support for learning, as they activate mental images that can help the language learner remember a particular structure or vocabulary item.
4. Pictures are more convenient than some realia to bring into the classroom (e.g., pictures of animals, burning buildings, outdoor activities, etc.).
5. Pictures add color and interest to discussions and writing exercises without being expensive or technologically top-heavy.
6. Pictures can be used in many ways by different teachers for various lessons. They are not tied to any particular teaching method, class size, or proficiency level. The same photograph can evoke many different kinds of language use in different contexts.
7. Pictures are convenient. They are easily transportable, light-weight, flat, and long-lasting (if properly mounted or laminated).
8. Pictures are very adaptable to the technology of the teaching environment (e.g., they can be scanned in, reworked and projected, or used where even electricity is unavailable).
9. Pictures can promote creative and critical thinking (for instance, in describing an everyday object photographed from an unusual angle, or clouds which appear to be different things to different people).
10. Finally, pictures are not limited to use with a particular language. Hence a picture file can be a valuable departmental resource in a context where several languages are taught.

Do you agree or disagree with the ten statements above? Put a plus (+) next to those you agree with, a minus (-) where you disagree, and a question mark (?) by the ones you're not sure about. Can you imagine other reasons to use pictures in a speaking class? Think about working with beginning learners in particular.

Here is a simple picture-based activity that works well with beginning students. Choose several different photographs that are quite similar but have some distinguishing features. For instance, I have a set of twelve large-format calendar photos of beautiful shells. With beginning students you can pre-teach the vocabulary that would be used to describe the shells and write the key words on the board. You can use category headings (size, shape, color, etc.) as well as individual lexical items (*big, small, tiny* for size; *round, flat, pointed, sharp* for shapes, and so on). Place all the photographs on the board with numbers above them. Pass out numbers to the individual students, but have them hide their numbers. (If you are working with calendar photos and have saved the small photographs from the back of the calendar, pass out these smaller versions to individual students and have them keep the photos hidden from their classmates.) Then one by one, each student describes the shell in his picture, while the others guess which one is being described. Write the name of the student whose picture the class has guessed above that picture, but don't reveal the right answers until everyone has had a chance to describe his own picture.

For a second round, you can cover or erase the vocabulary words from the board. This step encourages students to try to remember the words. If they have trouble recalling specific vocabulary items, you can put up parts of the word (e.g., "poin__" for *pointed*).

Action

Create a picture description activity using large-format photographs from calendars or magazines. Write the procedures for the activity, including specific instructions for the learners to follow. Try out the activity with a classmate or colleague before using it with a group of learners.

You can also create a competition with picture-based activities. I have a great set of photographs that are unrelated but have certain similarities. There are four sets of these photos and they are laminated so that I can use them over and over again. Each sheet contains twelve small photographs, including a picture of the earth taken from space, a boot, birds on a wire, books in a library, lightning crackling through the night sky, a map of Italy, a cracked pattern of lines in dried mud, an aerial view of a freeway interchange in Los Angeles, the tail fins of an automobile, a peacock's feather, a fly's eye, and so on. I have used these pictures with groups of beginning students and false beginners to do a task in which the students must find the similarities between two pictures. Here are the steps:

1. You may want to pre-teach phrases of comparison such as "X is like Y because…." or "X looks like Y" or "X and Y are both…" or "X and Y are similar because…."
2. Put the students in groups of three or four, and give each group a sheet of pictures. Each group must have the same pictures. (If you don't have a set of identical small-format photographs for each group, you can use large-format photos posted around the classroom or set in the chalk tray, as long as all the students can see every photograph.)
3. With the class as a whole, locate some of the obvious comparisons and practice using the structures in comparing the photos—for example, "The map of Italy looks like a boot."
4. Give the groups about five minutes to brainstorm several similarities in the photographs.
5. When the students have identified several comparisons, you can begin the whole class activity by calling on the groups in sequence. Each group is a team, and the teams get one point for every novel, legitimate comparison they make.
6. The point about novel comparisons is important. It forces the groups to listen to one another's contributions. In fact, I have even implemented the step of subtracting a point if a team repeats the same comparison that was given earlier by another team.
7. The game ends when you run out of time or when no teams can offer additional, novel comparisons.

In using this activity—even with very low-level learners—I have often been astounded at the clever comparisons the students make. For example, some have noted that the pattern on the peacock's feather is an eye—similar to the fly's eye. They have said that the cracks in the dried mud look like the lightning forking across the sky. The birds on the wire are lined up like the rows of books in the library. And inevitably these comparisons (and the excitement of the competition) cause them to ask vocabulary questions so they can express themselves and win points for their team (for example, they ask about the vocabulary for *lightning, mud, wire, peacock, feather,* and so on).

These are just a few of the speaking activities you can do with a collection of photographs in a class of beginning level students. In addition, a single photograph can be used for many different activities. I encourage new teachers to begin building a collection of colorful photos, whether you get them out of recycled magazines, out-of-date calendars, or from the Internet. They are a very valuable (and cheap!) resource for promoting speaking in the classroom.

In case you would like to collect some photographs to use in your classes, here are ten steps to building a language learning picture file:

1. Collect large, high quality colored pictures from calendars and magazines. Travel brochures, catalogs, and advertising literature are also quite helpful.

2. Flip through the magazines and calendars, tearing out pictures that you like for their color, action, composition, emotional appeal, etc. Or print out pictures from the Internet. There is no need to cut them or carefully trim them at this point.

3. Collect lightweight cardboard, including the single sheets of grey cardboard that come in packaged stationery goods. Offices that use many paper products throw these away, and stationery stores sometimes give them away for free. (Corrugated cardboard is sturdy, but it takes up too much space in storage. Manila file folders are a bit too flimsy and tend to fall apart after a few years.)

4. Buy one small jar and one large can of rubber cement, which is much cheaper when bought in bulk. The small jar contains the applicator brush and can be refilled easily from the large can.

5. When you have several pictures and lots of cardboard saved, apply a thin coat of rubber cement first to a piece of cardboard, and then to the back of the picture you wish to mount.

6. Press the sticky sides of the picture and the cardboard together and smooth out any ripples with your hands or with a roller. Repeat steps 1 through 6 for as many pictures as you want.

7. Press the pictures overnight under a large book or heavy box. This step seals the rubber cement and ensures a smooth surface. Pressing the pictures this way helps to prevent the pictures from separating from the mounting material later.

(I actually have some mounted pictures that have held up through twenty years of classroom use.)

8. Trim the edges of the mounted pictures using a large paper cutter with a sharp blade. After trimming, check for stray spots of rubber cement. By this time it will be dry but tacky and can easily be rolled off the picture's surface with your fingertips.

9. File the pictures according to topical categories: people, animals, action shots, buildings, food and beverages, vehicles, scenery, etc. (If you file them according to their intended teaching uses, such as mass vs. count nouns or comparison and contrast, you may not imagine using them for anything else.)

10. If this is a communal picture file to be used by many people, keep a notebook nearby where teachers can record brief notes about what they have done with the various pictures. This step will help prevent accidental overlap, so the students don't feel they have been made to repeat lessons. It may also inspire other teachers to try out their colleagues' ideas or to come up with creative ideas of their own.

Adapted from Curtis and Bailey, 2001

If you have access to a laminating machine, you can skip steps 3 through 8. You also can work with PowerPoint presentations or other means of projecting photographs (for instance, with color photocopies as transparencies).

6. Physical actions in speaking lessons

Activities involving physical actions can help learners remember the meaning of words and structures. Such activities help you, as the teacher, see whether or not students have understood directions, tasks, or commands. They provide a way for low-level learners to respond without speaking (or in addition to speaking). They can also break up the possible tedium of sitting still in classrooms for long periods of time.

Reflection

When you have studied a new language, did your teachers use physical activities to help you learn? If so, what was your reaction to those activities? Did they make learning memorable?

In **Total Physical Response (TPR)**, students learn by associating physical actions with the language they are hearing (Asher, Kusoda, and de la Torre, 1993). It is a comprehension-based approach to learning, but it can be utilized in teaching and practicing speaking as well. The "total" in Total Physical Response refers to the idea that students retain in memory those things they use their whole bodies to do. Indeed many TPR activities involve students standing and moving. In other activities the students remain seated, but move objects as they follow the commands to do the task.

A typical TPR activity resembles the children's game of "Simon Says," in which a leader gives verbal commands (Simon says touch your nose, Simon says stand on your left foot, Simon says close your eyes, etc.) that the listeners are supposed to follow *if* and *only if* the leader says, "Simon says…." TPR activities don't include the obligatory "Simon says" opener, but a leader does give verbal commands to others to follow.

The key here in using TPR activities in a speaking class is for the teacher to quickly get the students into the role of giving the commands. After demonstrating the activity with a round of commands, the teacher can turn the leader's role over to the students and have them give the directions. TPR activities can be used for practicing many grammatical structures and vocabulary items in the oral mode. But activities don't have to include total body movement in order to be useful and memorable.

Here is a beginning-level physical response activity using colored paper. You can begin with a very simple set of materials and then build on them. Give each student a red triangle, a red circle, a red square, and a red rectangle. Elicit the names for each shape. If the vocabulary appears to be new for some students, write it on the board next to a drawing of the shape. As the teacher running the activity, you'll have a set of the same materials the students have.

Start with simple commands with your pieces of paper showing, so the students can see them. As you give the commands the first few times, you do what you are telling the students to do in plain view so the learners can check their understanding of the task and the language. Here is an example sequence: "Put the red triangle on the desk. Put the circle on top of the triangle. Put the square on top of the circle. Put the rectangle on top of the square." (Check to see if everyone has followed these directions.) "Okay, everyone? Please pick up the rectangle. Now pick up the square. Next pick up the circle. Pick up the triangle." (All the papers should be removed now.) "Let's try it again. Put the rectangle on the desk. Put the circle on the rectangle. Put the square on the rectangle. Now PICK UP the rectangle. Put the triangle on the square. Now put the rectangle on the triangle." (Have the students check with their neighbors to see if they have done the sequence correctly.)

At this point you can build in a step where you repeat the commands listed above, but with your own papers hidden from the students so they cannot check their understanding by comparing their paper stacks to yours. Or, if you feel the students are getting the idea (or if the classroom is so big or so crowded they can't see your example anyway), have them work in pairs. (If you have movable desks or chairs, this is an ideal activity for using tango seating.) Student A builds a sequence of paper shapes, using simple commands to describe it, while Student B builds the sequence Student A is describing. Afterwards, they compare their paper shape sequences. Then they switch roles and Student B gives the commands while Student A follows the instructions, again using tango seating.

When the students have mastered the names of the shapes and have the idea of how the activity works, give them a new set of papers–for instance, a green triangle, square, circle, and rectangle. When you feel they are ready, add blue and yellow shapes as well. Eventually each person will have four different shapes each in four (or more) different colors. You can make the activity as elaborate as you like. While you are giving instructions and the students are responding to them, it is primarily a listening activity, but when the students take turns giving the commands, it is both a speaking and listening activity.

The activity described thus far has just been used to teach and practice the names of colors and shapes. But this kind of command-based procedure can be useful for teaching and practicing many other things as well. For instance, all of the examples above use the commands, "Put the [noun] on top of the [noun]" or "Pick up the [noun]." But several different prepositions and many more verbs can be used in this exercise as well.

Action

Make a list of at least eight prepositions that would be useful for beginning and false-beginning students to know, and which could be used in a TPR activity like this one. Here are a few to help you get started:

1. Over
2.
3. Above
4.
5. To the left of
6.
7. In front of
8.

Can you think of others? It may be helpful for you to manipulate the paper pieces while a classmate or colleague describes what you are doing. Together you may come up with prepositions that you have not thought of yourself.

Next make a list of verbs that could be introduced in this activity. Choose high-frequency verbs that would be useful for beginning and false-beginning students to know. For example, you can start with *put*, but gradually add new vocabulary, such as *cover* or *hide*: "cover the circle with the rectangle."

A useful TPR activity for beginning students and false beginners has to do with following verbal directions from one place to another. You can start with a listening exercise for the whole class and then convert it to a speaking activity.

Begin with the students standing by their desks or tables. Start with commands of position: "Turn left, turn right, face north (east, south, west); look up, look down, look left, look right, take two steps forward, take one step backward, go to the window, go to the door," and so on. Depending on the physical layout of your classroom, you can work with the whole group, or divide the class in half and have the two halves face outward, with one student giving commands to each half. You must decide what will work the best, given the space in your classroom, the number of students, and the point of the lesson. Practice the TPR commands for a brief period of time—three or four minutes—until it appears that all the students are correctly matching their physical actions to the verbal commands. Then have the students get into groups of three to five people. One student gives the commands while the others act on them.

You can turn this TPR activity into a version of hide-and-seek if you wish. Start with some small object (such as an envelope) that can be easily hidden. If you have a relatively small class (say, thirty or fewer students) you can send one student out of the room for a minute. This person is the seeker. Hide the envelope (e.g., in the lower left drawer of the teacher's desk). Divide the remaining students into two teams—one group that is supporting the seeker's efforts and one that interferes with his efforts to find the envelope. The seeker, however, doesn't know which of his classmates are helping and which are hindering his efforts to find the prize. It works well if you have each student take a number in sequence by counting aloud. Then have the even numbered students support the seeker and the odd numbered students try to prevent him from finding the hidden object.

When the seeker re-enters the room, his classmates begin to give him instructions, but you need to set up some ground rules so that no one simply tells him, "Look in the left drawer of the teacher's desk." For instance, you could say that each command can only involve motion in the space of two feet (about half a meter). So for example, his classmates could say, "Take one step to the front of the room," but not "Walk to the teacher's desk." Those on the thwarting side can say things such as "look out the window" or "face the back of the room." As the teacher, you must call on people from around the room to take turns, intermingling clues from supporters with clues from thwarters, to make sure the competition is fair and that everyone gets a chance to speak.

5. Teaching pronunciation

One key to success in learning to speak a foreign language is having good pronunciation. It is not at all necessary for students to sound like native speakers (though some may have that goal). It is important, however, to be comprehensible. In order to help learners improve their pronunciation, it is important to understand some important information about how the sounds of English are produced.

In Chapter 1 (p. 11) we saw that the vowels and consonants are the segmental phonemes of English. Vowels are produced when the air stream passing through the vocal chords is shaped but not obstructed. The following diagram shows the sixteen key vowel phonemes of English and common English words which exemplify the particular vowel in the box.

1 **see** / iy / 2 **it** / I /		13 **two** / uw / 12 **books** /ʊ/
3 **say** / ey / 4 **yes** / e /	14 **about** /ə/	11 **no** / ow / 10 **boy** / oy /
5 **fat** / æ /	6 **my** / ay / 8 **cow** / aw / 7 **stop** / a /	9 **law** /ɔ/

Figure 1 Symbols for 16 vowel phonemes and key words (adapted from Murphy, 2003, p. 123)

Say the words in the vowel chart in Figure 1 (p. 65) aloud in order of their numbers. That is, start with (1) *see* and finish with (14) *about*. As you speak, pay attention to where in your mouth each particular vowel sound is being produced. Having done that, what do you think the layout of the vowel chart is supposed to represent?

As you can see from the above Reflection box, different vowel sounds are produced at different places in the mouth. In fact, the chart above is often superimposed on a profile of a face, looking to the left. The vowel sounds in *see, it, say, yes,* and *fat* are called the "front vowels" because they are produced at the front of the mouth. The vowels in *my, stop,* and *cow* are called the "mid-vowels" and those in *law, boy, no, books,* and *two* are called the "back vowels," because they are produced at the back of the mouth.

The sound in the first syllable of *about* is called the "schwa." It is represented as /ə/ in most phonemic symbol systems. This sound, which is the mid-central vowel, is very important in English because it occurs in many un-stressed syllables, regardless of a word's spelling. Here is an explanation about the schwa sound for learners of English. This is a very important and pervasive sound in spoken language.

Example 9

PRONUNCIATION Activities

The /ə/ Sound in Unstressed Syllables

You have learned that English words have stressed and unstressed syllables. You know that stressed syllables have longer, louder, and higher sounds than unstressed syllables. When native speakers of English pronounce the sounds in unstressed syllables quickly and quietly, the vowel sound in these syllables often changes to the sound /ə/. This sound is called the *schwa* sound.

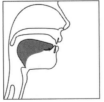

This sound is made by relaxing your tongue in the middle of your mouth. It sounds like the sound "uh." The /ə/ sound occurs in most unstressed syllables, but you can also find it in some stressed syllables in words like *bug, money, stuff.* In this lesson, however, you will practice /ə/ only in unstressed syllables.

Talk It Up! Oral Communication for the Real World (Kozyrev, 1998. p. 29)

Action

Say the following words aloud to yourself: *rug, the, above, done.* You can see that regardless of the spelling, each of these vowels (except the silent E's at the end of *above* and *done*) are pronounced as the schwa sound (ə). Now say the following phrases aloud:

the apple	the pear	the airplane	the ship
the ant	the bug	the idea	the thought

How is the vowel sound in the word *the* pronounced if the following word begins with a consonant? What if the following word begins with a vowel?

The consonant phonemes are also produced at various places in the mouth. When consonants are produced, unlike vowels, the air stream that passes through the vocal chords is obstructed and is strongly influenced by the different parts of the mouth. When that happens we talk about the **place of articulation**.

Reflection

Look at the following chart of the consonants in Figure 2. Underline any words you do not know and cannot guess. Some of the symbols in the consonant chart look like regular English letters, while other symbols are not so familiar. Can you figure out what sound each symbol represents?

	Place of Articulation													
Manner of Articulation	Bilabial		Labiodental		Interdental		Alveolar		Palatal		Velar		Glottal	
Stop	p	b					t	d			k	g	?	
Fricative			f	v	θ	ð	s	z	š	ž			h	
Affricate									č	ǰ				
Nasal		m						n				ŋ		
Lateral Liquid								l						
Retroflex Liquid								r						
Glide	w̥	w								y				

State of the Glottis: Voiceless | Voiced

Figure 2 Place and manner of articulation (Stewart and Vaillete, 2001, p. 46)

The place of articulation refers to where in the vocal tract speech sounds are actually produced. If you read the column headings on the chart above from left to right, you will see that they refer to parts of your mouth, starting with the lips and working toward the throat. Some of the vocabulary in this chart can be interpreted if you know the base words (for instance, *labial* refers to the lips and *dental* to the teeth), and look at the phonemes in the columns.

Reflection

Try to figure out the meanings of *bilabial, labiodental,* and *interdental* by making the following sounds.

bilabial: /p/, /b/, /m/, /w/
labiodental: /f/, /v/
interdental: /θ/, /ð/,

(Hint: /θ/ is the first sound in *thought* and /ð/ is the first sound in *that*.)

Some of the other vocabulary items in this chart are not so easy to figure out, but they all deal with where sounds are produced. Alveolar sounds are made when the tip of the tongue touches the **alveolar ridge**, the uneven surface on the roof of your mouth just behind your upper front teeth. The palatal sounds are made at the hard palate, the smooth area behind the alveolar ridge on the roof of the mouth. Finally, the glottal sounds are made at the glottis, in the very back of the mouth.

These are the phonemes of English, but other languages have important sounds that English lacks, and English has some sounds (like /θ/ and /ð/), which are not common in other languages.

The left column of the consonant chart lists several different ways in which consonants are produced. This is called the **manner of articulation.** The phrase "manner of articulation" simply refers to how sounds are produced. For instance, in some English sounds (/p/, /b/, /t/, /d/, /k/, and /g/) the air stream is temporarily stopped. In others, the air stream is partially obstructed, creating a kind of friction (as in the **fricatives**–/f/, /v/, /θ/, / ð /, /s/, /z/, /š/, /ž/, and /h/). In two others, the affricates– /č/ and / ǰ /–the air is momentarily stopped and then released with friction.

In making other sounds the air stream is not so firmly obstructed. For example, there are two "liquid" sounds–/l/ and /r/–which are produced at the sides of the mouth and the back of the mouth, respectively, giving them the points of articulation we call "lateral" and "retroflex." And in producing the "glides"–/w̥/, /w/, and /y/–the articulators glide from one sound to another. You can understand the meaning of "glides" if you say "away" and stretch out the /w/ sound. **Glides** are sounds that serve as transitions between two vowel sounds. When glides are produced the vocal tract is "only slightly more constricted than that for vowels" (Stewart and Vaillette, 2001, p. 494). Throughout this book we will talk about the place of articulation and manner of articulation as we discuss how teachers can help learners improve their pronunciation.

Another important group of segmental phonemes are called **"affricates"**–that is, the / ǰ / sound at the beginning and end of the word *judge,* and the /č/ sound at the beginning and end of the word *church.* The affricates consist of a stop followed immediately by a fricative. The /j/ sound is really a quick combination of /d/ and /ž/, while the / ǰ / sound consists of /t/ followed quickly by /š/.

Say the following words aloud to yourself slowly and analyze the affricates as you produce them. Be aware of both the place and manner of articulation as you do so.

Chapel	Bir**ch**	**J**est	Knowle**dge**
Check	Bat**ch**	**J**ury	Ri**dge**
Cheek	Tha**tch**	**J**et	Bu**dge**

Cheese	**Cru**tch	**J**ust	**Gru**dge
Chest	**Wi**tch	**J**ewelry	**Refri**gerator

You can see that in some instances the word's spelling accurately reflects the way these phonemes are produced. In other words, it does not.

Affricates appear as phonemes in words, as shown in this Action box. They are also produced in rapid, casual speech, when words blend together (e.g., when "What do you want?" is pronounced as "Watcha want?"). Here's how the process of reduced speech is explained and exemplified in a textbook for beginning students and false beginners:

Example 10

> ### Reduced Forms in Questions with *Do* and *Did* (Audio)
>
> When people speak quickly, some words become reduced, or short. Here are some examples.
>
> | Long Form | Short Form |
> |---|---|
> | *Why do you* want that? | Why'dya want that? |
> | *What do you* mean? | Wha'dya mean? |
> | *What did you* say? | Wha'ja say? |
> | *Where did you* say you were going? | Where'ja say you were going? |
> | *Who did you* speak to? | Who'ja speak to? |
> | *When did you* leave? | When'ja leave? |
> | *How did you* get here? | How'ja get here? |

Quest: Listening and Speaking in the Academic World, Book One
(Hartmann and Blass, 2000, p. 133)

Say the following sentences aloud quickly, without trying to be precise or careful as you speak.

1. What do you want to do?
2. Where do you want to go?
3. Why did you choose that place?
4. When did you get home?
5. How did you like the movie?

As you say these sentences, listen to the way the sounds get reduced. In the space to the right of each sentence, write the utterance as it is pronounced in casual speech.

It is often the case that pronunciation issues interact with grammar issues. As a result, if learners mispronounce key sounds, it can seem like they are producing ungrammatical utterances.

One very important grammar point that beginning learners and false beginners often work on is the past tense and other cases were verbs end in *–ed*. Depending on the surrounding sounds, the *–ed* ending can be pronounced in three different ways. Here is an explanation and some examples from a textbook for beginning students and false beginner students:

Example 11

UNIT 9 *-ed* endings

A. 🎧 Listen to the examples. Listen again and repeat them.

walked /t/   dreamed /d/   started /ed/

B. 🎧 Do you hear /t/, /d/, or /ed/? Listen and check [✓].

	/t/	/d/	/ed/
1. listened			
2. stopped			
3. watched			
4. needed			
5. played			
6. checked			
7. exercised			
8. wanted			

C. Practice the conversations below with a partner.

1. A: Did you drive here?
B: No, I walked.

2. A: What time did you start?
B: I started at about 3:00.

3. A: What did you do last night?
B: Oh, I just listened to music.

4. A: Why did you go to the store?
B: I needed some bread.

5. A: What did you do last night?
B: Nothing special. I watched a boring movie on TV.

6. A: Did you have fun yesterday?
B: Yes! I played baseball with my friends.

ICON Intro International Communication Through English (Freeman, Graves, and Lee, 2005, p. 90)

Also, particularly for beginning learners in EFL situations, and especially for those who have had mostly reading exposure to English (and not much listening exposure), there is sometimes a tendency to pronounce the *-ed* as if it were a syllable no matter where it occurs. For instance, students may correctly say "hunted" as two syllables, but then also say "roped" as "ro-ped" or "pulled" as "pul-led" because the spelling suggests that *-ed* is a syllable to be said.

For learners whose native language doesn't use consonant clusters (see Chapter 1, page 11) at the end of words, pronouncing the English past tense and other *-ed* endings can be very difficult. It will take some practice on the learners' part and some explanation on yours.

If you work with (or plan to work with) students from a particular first-language background, it can be very helpful to know what contrastive analysis predicts those learners' challenges will be—particularly in the area of pronunciation (and especially for adult learners). Go online or visit a university library and look for any contrastive analyses that have been written about English and the native language of your students. (If you have, or will have, students from varied first language backgrounds, choose a language that you are not familiar with.)

6. Speaking in the classroom

In this section, we will consider how teachers deal with speaking in the classroom. The following transcript is from an actual lesson with a group of false beginning students in an EFL context. The teacher uses a number of verbal strategies to check the students' understanding and get them to speak. He also has the students work in pairs, and the task in the book provides them with something to talk about. In Extract 1, *T* stands for teacher, *Ss* stands for students.

> **Extract 1**
>
> **T:** *Have a look at Task 4 on page 3. You'll see some words. Two lists of words that're used for describing people. Just look through them, and just put a check mark next to the words you know as I read them through.* [T reads list as Ss check words they know.] *OK, just, just compare with your partner to see if there are any words that you didn't know there.*
>
> **Ss:** [Inaudible.]

T: Very difficult, eh? [Laughter.] OK, the next task, the next task is slightly more difficult. One of the things, er, we practice in this course.. is.. or some of the things we practice are learning strategies. And one of the learning strategies that will help you learn new words is the learning strategy of "classifying." Do you know what "classifying" means?

Ss: No, no.

T: Have you heard this word before?

Ss: No.

T: Classifying means putting things that are similar together in groups. OK? So if I said, er, I want all the girls to go down to that corner of the room, and all the boys to go into this corner of the room, I would be classifying the class according to their sex or their gender. What I'd like you to do now in Task 5 is to classify some of the words from the list in Task 4. OK? [Ss carry out task as T writes headings on board.]

Adapted from Nunan and Lamb, 1996, pp. 259-261

Reflection

Study the instructional sequence in Extract 1. What is the main point being taught? How is it being taught? How old do you think the learners are?

The lesson which started in Extract 1 continues below in Extract 2. It begins when the teacher asks the students if they have finished their pairwork, in which they classified the words from the list.

Extract 2

T: Finished?

Ss: Yes.

T: OK. Someone like to call out the color words for me please.

S: Dark.

T: Yeah, interesting. Is "dark" a color?

Ss: [Inaudible.]

T: Is dark a color?

S: [Inaudible.]

T: *Let's put it in anyway.* [Writes on board.] *OK. Next one?*

Ss: *White, white.*

T: [Writes on board.] *Next one?*

Ss: *Blue.*

T: [Writes on board.] *And?*

Ss: *Blond.*

T: *Blond.* [Writes on board.] *What about the "age" words?*

S: *Eld........*

T: *How do you say that word? How do you pronounce that word?*

Ss: *Elderly.*

T: *Next one?*

Ss: [Inaudible.]

T: [Writes on board.] *Next one?*

Ss: *Old.*

T: [Writes on board] *Next one?*

Ss: *Middle aged.*

T: [Writes on board.] *And the last one?*

Ss: *Teenage.*

T: [Writes on board.] *OK. And the last list? Size. Big?*

Ss: *Short.*

T: *Uh-huh.*

Ss: *Tall.*

T: *Uh-huh.*

Ss: *Small.*

T: *Right. What's the difference between this word* [points to "elderly"] *and this word* [points to "old"]*? Elderly and old? Does anybody know the difference?*

S: *I know in Japanese.*

T: *You can't explain in Japanese, because I wouldn't understand.*

Ss: [Laughter.]

Adapted from Nunan and Lamb, 1996, pp. 261-262

What is the point being taught in Extract 2? How is it being taught? Which of the principles from Section 3 is the teacher using?

In Extracts 1 and 2, the students speak mostly in single-word utterances, while the teacher uses longer, more complex utterances. Yet it appears that the students understand the teacher's speech. What evidence can you find in these extracts that the students do understand and are following the lesson? What are the different ways the teacher helps the students understand and do the task? What are three strategies the teacher uses to encourage the students to speak? Underline those strategies in Extracts 1 and 2.

In Extract 3, the teacher explains the difference between *elderly* and *old*. He then leads the students into the next part of the lesson, which involves listening for key words and phrases in a recorded conversation.

Extract 3

T: If I said that, um, that Mr. Smith was elderly, but Mr. Jones was old, I think that probably I would imagine that old, someone who's old, is slightly older than someone who is elderly. Elderly also is slightly more polite. To say that someone is elderly it doesn't sound quite as, quite as very direct as if you say that somebody is old.... Although I'm not sure. I'd have to check with some other native speakers [Laughter]. How would you describe yourself? How would you describe yourself? I would say that I'm, well in my culture, I guess I'm short. I'm fairly short. I used to like living in Asia because I was very big there. I was tall cause most people in [Asia] are about that tall. [Gestures.]

Ss: [Laughter.]

T: I wouldn't say I was elderly. I guess I'm middle-aged. I used to have blond hair, but now it's gone a kind of dirty brown, and is going gray. OK. Over the page, then. These are some of the things we're going to be practicing this morning. I'm going to ask you to listen to another conversation now. And I'm going to play the conversation three or four times. The first time, I just want you to listen and to check off the words in Task 1 when you hear them. OK? Just listen for these words and I'm going to ask you if you actually hear these words, 'cause they *may not all be on the tape. So the first time you listen I just want you to check off these words. Do you know the meaning of all these words? "last name," "first name," "address," "telephone number," "date of birth," "occupation," and "marital status." Do you know the meaning of all of those words?*

S: What word is "occupation"?

T: Sorry?

S: What is "occupation"?

T: Occupation. Can anybody tell, explain what "occupation" is?

S: Work.

S: [Inaudible.]

T: Sorry?

Ss: [Inaudible.] Work.

T: Yes. What sort of job that someone does. What sort of job. Or what work that somebody does. What about "marital status"? Do you know that word? That phrase?

Ss: No, no.

T: That simply means are you married or single or divorced or widowed. OK. Do you have a husband or wife? Or are you single? Or are you divorced? So if somebody asks you your marital status. So if somebody asks you "What's your marital status?" You would say "I'm ..? .... single. I'm single." OK, let's listen to the next conversation.

Adapted from Nunan and Lamb, 1996, pp. 262-264

This listening exercise could clearly lead to a speaking activity in which one student interviews another and fills out a form with information about his partner. If these questions are culturally appropriate in your context, they could also be the basis of a contact assignment in which your learners interview people other than their classmates.

Design a form with topics and blank lines that your beginning students could use as a guide for interviewing one another during in-class pairwork.

Next, write the instructions for a contact assignment in which learners (perhaps working in pairs) would interview other people in English and write down the information they learn.

7. Assessing beginning learners

There are many different reasons for assessing the speaking skills of beginning learners or false beginners. Often students are given a test as they enter a program of instruction to see what level class they should join. Unless students are true beginning level students starting with the very first course, such **placement tests** can be very useful in providing information about which course students should take as they begin to study English in a new program.

Once students are enrolled in classes, individual teachers often use **diagnostic tests** to see what students already know and what they still need to learn in terms of the syllabus of that particular course. **Progress tests** are used during a course to see how well students have mastered particular parts of the material, while **achievement tests** are used at the end of a course of instruction to see if students have learned the skills and content covered in that class. Diagnostic, progress, and achievement tests are used by some independent learning, centers as well.

In this section, we will first see how a fun introductory activity can be used as a diagnostic measure of students' speaking abilities. We will also look at a text that was written specifically to elicit particular phonemes, as a way of locating students' pronunciation difficulties. Finally, we will consider propositional scoring for determining students' skill at conveying meaning.

1. Class introductions: Icebreaker and speaking assessment

An icebreaker is an activity used to get people (especially strangers) to feel comfortable talking to one another. Icebreakers can be very helpful in speaking classes.

Here is a very simple diagnostic procedure that I use for the first day of class no matter what level students I am teaching. It can be adapted to make it more or less difficult, or to accommodate larger or smaller class sizes. The beauty of the exercise is that it functions as an icebreaker and helps the students get to know one another. Typically they have no idea that you are assessing their speaking skills. Here's how it works:

1. Give every student a 3" x 5" index card or similar piece of paper.
2. Each student neatly prints his or her full name on the card and you then collect all the cards.
3. Redistribute the cards to the students, making sure no one has his or her own card. Ideally, the student shouldn't know the person whose card he or she receives. Keep one student's card for yourself and include a card with your name on it among those you distribute.

4. Write on the board: Name, name to be called in class, three things he/she likes, three things he/she dislikes.

5. Have all the students stand up and find the person whose card they have. (They need to take a pen or pencil along with the card.) This phase of the activity generates a lot of talk and milling around and takes a while, since they are not paired up as partners. For example, you have Jong Kim's card, but he may have Jose Garcia's card, and Jose has Mieko Funabashi's card.)

6. Each student interviews the person whose name is on his or her card, making brief notes on the card. Watch the students and after about 3 to 5 minutes, advise them that they need to finish up and move on to their next discussion. That is, it is now their turn to interview or be interviewed, whichever part of the task they have not done yet. The activity continues until everyone has been interviewed once and has conducted one interview.

7. As they finish, the students resume their seats. (I like using this procedure for classroom management: You can have students do brief speaking activities while standing and then have them sit down as they finish. This action shows you and the rest of the class who is done and when a particular phase of the activity is drawing to a close. It also breaks the monotony of sitting.)

8. When all the students are seated, you begin the introductions by saying, "Good morning everyone! This is Jong Kim. He wants to be called Jong. He likes tennis, movies, and sleeping late. He doesn't like studying."

9. Then Jong Kim comes to the front of the room and introduces Jose Garcia. As Jong speaks about Jose, you make notes on Jong's card about his English speaking skills.

10. Next you take Jose's card from Jong Kim and make notes on the back of Jose's card about Jose's speaking as he introduces Mieko Funabashi. Take Mieko's card from Jose and make notes on the back of it about Mieko's English as she introduces Panita Niminit, the person whose card she had, and so on.

If you have plenty of time and/or a small class of lower level students you can add more questions. For example, in an ESL class, you can have the students find out what country their classmates are from. In an EFL class, you can have them find out what part of the city their classmates live in, which secondary school they attended, what train station they use, or which dormitory they stay in. It is your job to select questions (or have the students suggest questions) which are age- and context-appropriate and which do not violate any social taboos in the culture where you are working.

Extract 4 provides some examples of students' speech from false beginners and lower-intermediate students doing the introduction activity described above. These data are compiled from my memories of many years of using this activity, rather than from transcripts of actual audio recordings.

> ### Extract 4
>
> 1. **Jong Kim's speech:** *Uh, okay. Good morning. Uh, this Jose Garcia. He like Jose. Uhm—in class* [pauses], *he name Jose. He like eat* [pauses], *he like to eat, and, uh, sleeping, like me* [laughter from the class], *and uh, he like car. His car. No, no* [pauses]—*he want to have his car. And he not like people talk English. Uh, no! He not like people talk English fast.*
>
> 2. **Jose Garcia's speech:** *Okay, so, hello, and this my friend Meko. Is right, Meko?"* (Mieko laughs and shakes her head.) *"How you say?"* (Mieko says, "Mi-e-ko!", stressing the three syllables; [laughter from the class].) *Jose continues, "Oh, yeah, okay, Mi-e-ko"* [stressing three syllables—more laughter from the class]. *"Mieko, she like chopping, chopping the clothes"* [laughter from the class as Mieko shakes her head], *"no es right chopping?"* (Mieko and others say "ssshhhh" and "shopping.") *Jose says, "Oh, yeah—I know. Chopping is* [gestures chopping with the side of his hand] *es 'ch.' Okay, she like ssshhhopping* [exaggerated /š/ sound] *the clothes"* [laughter from everyone, including Jose]. *"And she like also the, the, ¿como se dice? the food of Japan, the food Japanese, the sushi, and she like the dancing. And no like study the grammar of English, uh, the English grammar. That is all.*
>
> 3. **Mieko Funabashi's speech:** *Good morning, everybody. I am Mieko Funabashi. I am introduce Miss Panita Niminit. But she like her name is 'Nan' in class. So please say 'Nan.' Is her short name and friendly name, 'Nan.' Nan like many things. She like cooking Thailand food, so for class party she make Thailand food. And she like, uh, how can I say, she like shopping, and me too! I like shopping. And Nan, she is like, I mean she like play piano. But she not like, she don't like get up early in the morning. She like to sleep. So this is Nan.*

What can you determine about these three students' speaking skills from the brief extracts printed above? Based on just these speech samples, which of the three do you consider to be the least proficient speaker of English? The most proficient speaker? Write some comments about each student's strengths and weaknesses in spoken English. Include comments about their pronunciation, their grammar, and their apparent breadth of vocabulary, as well as their fluency in speaking English.

Here are my notes about each of these students. Remember that these comments were written on the back of a 3" x 5" card as the each student was introducing his or her classmate, so they are necessarily brief.

Notes on Jong Kim's speech: Greets class. No copula "be." No 3rd person singular S on "like." Says "he name Jose" (instead of "his name is Jose"). Self corrects "He like eat" to "he like to eat." But did say "his car" (instead of "he car"). Used "he not like"—may not have analyzed "do + not." Speech somewhat hesitant, but okay for level of class.

Notes on Jose Garcia's speech: Greets class. Lacks copula "be." Checks pronunciation of "Mieko." Good sense of humor. Seems confident. Self-corrects "chopping" to "shopping." Transfers adjective order from Spanish: "the food Japanese." Lacks 3rd person singular S and analyzed "do + not." Says "no like study." Finishes with "That is all." Maybe an unanalyzed chunk? Speech generally fluent and confident. May have idea of using communication strategies (risk-taking personality?).

Notes on Mieko Funabashi's speech: Greets class. Uses "I am" in introducing self. But also says, "I am introduce..." and "name is" (may have copula emerging). Lacks 3rd person singular S on "like." Uses plural S on "many things." Said "Thailand food" (instead of "Thai food"). Uses "how can I say?" (maybe a formulaic expression). Uses "so" and "me too." Says "like play piano" (missing infinitive "to" and article "the"). Says "she not like" but changes to "she don't like"—may have analyzed "do" and negation emerging. Knows "get up" and "early in the morning." Speech not hesitant. Pretty advanced for this class?

This classroom introduction activity can be used at the beginning of a course for you as the teacher to get a quick idea of each student's speaking proficiency. In addition, it will help you (and the students) to learn the class members' names and build a sense of community. Also, if you have time left after the introductions you can add a quick listening and speaking activity to help students remember one another's names. As Extract 5 shows you, simply ask questions about the information the students provided:

> **Extract 5**
>
> *T:* Who likes to play the piano?
>
> *Ss:* Mieko! No, no—Nan!
>
> *T:* Mieko told us that Nan likes to play the piano. Okay, who likes to sleep?
>
> *Ss:* Nan! No, Jose!
>
> *T:* Right! Nan likes to sleep. Jose likes to sleep. Nan and Jose both like to sleep. Who else likes to sleep? Someone else likes to sleep. Who was it? Do you remember?
>
> *Ss:* Jong Kim! Jong!
>
> *T:* That's right. Nan and Jose and Jong all like to sleep.

Notice that as the teacher in this extract coaches the students and summarizes what they have said, her speech provides model utterances that use correct English. She uses the students' ideas and elaborates upon them.

2. A pronunciation diagnostic test

A diagnostic test for evaluating a student's pronunciation can be written as a reading aloud task which incorporates the phonemes that contrastive analysis predicts would be troublesome for students from a given first language background. (A **contrastive analysis** is a systematic comparison of the students' first language with English to determine the differences that will need attention during instruction. It can be conducted at the levels of phonology, morphology, lexicon, syntax, or discourse.) For example, the following passage was written for Spanish speakers learning English. If you are familiar with Spanish, you will see that many of the consonants and vowels in this text are those that are often problematic for Spanish speakers of English.

Example 11

> Buddy always pulled up a chair to watch his father wash and shave. He saw him spread the hot lather with a wet, yellow brush and then zip off the whiskers with a cheap razor that looked just like tin to him. Buddy would wait to see if the thin blade cut his father's face, yet it never did. Sometimes his father would even sing in his gravely voice as he pulled the sharp razor across his skin. Once Buddy thought he spotted blood and was thrilled. But later he felt bad because he was sure it was a sin to have these thoughts.

Galvan, Pierce, and Underwood, 1976, p. 20

When you use a passage like this to assess a learner's pronunciation, the learner reads the passage aloud into a tape recorder. Later you can score the reading by marking a clean copy of the passage for each student, circling the phonemes that were mispronounced. If you print the passage in a double-spaced format, you can write in the sounds the learner substituted for the English phonemes. This information will show you some ways to help the students improve their pronunciation.

There are some points to keep in mind, however, if you use read-aloud passages as testing texts. First, if what you wish to assess is the learners' pronunciation, then the text itself should not be demanding, relative to the learners' proficiency, in terms of the vocabulary or syntactic structures it involves. You should answer the students' questions about word meanings and pronunciation of any new words before they read the passage on tape, because the text is meant to be a test of accentedness—not of reading skills. Also, be aware that people can sometimes be more conscientious about their pronunciation accuracy when they are reading aloud than when they are trying to generate novel utterances of their own.

Action

Write a brief paragraph that incorporates the vowel and consonants sounds of English that pose particular problems for your learners, if you are already teaching (or for those students you hope to work with in the future, if you are not). The text should sound natural and should include only words and grammatical structures that your learners are likely to know. (This is a pronunciation task—not a test of reading or of how students interpret new words in context.) Type the text in double-spaced format so it will be easier for the learners to read (and for you to mark later) than if it were single-spaced. Have a few of your colleagues or classmates read it aloud for you on tape before you try using it with students.

I suggest that you *not* use "tongue-twisters" as the basis for testing students' pronunciation. While the texts of tongue-twisters can be fun (and funny) as in-class exercises, even native speakers have trouble saying them aloud (that's the whole point!), so it is not appropriate to score lower-level learners on a task that native or proficient non-native speakers cannot do easily and well.

If you are working with preliterate students, instead of having them read a passage aloud, you can ask them to repeat after you. This task is called **sentence repetition** and it provides comparable data across the various students. Like the reading described above, however, it can be a bit impractical if you have to administer the task to individual students—especially in large classes. Be sure to audio-record the students' utterances so you can score them (or analyze them) later. It can be distracting to you and very intimidating to the learners if you are obviously scoring their speech at the same time you are testing them.

3. Propositional scoring for assessing meaning in speech

Propositional scoring is a procedure for assessing the meaning conveyed by an utterance (see Bailey, 1998) rather than grammatical accuracy. A **proposition** is the basic meaning(s) of a sentence or utterance. For example, in the following sentence, there are four propositions:

My friend Scott teaches English in Romania.

1. I have a friend.
2. My friend's name is Scott.
3. He teaches English.
4. He teaches in Romania.

Determine the number of propositions in this utterance:
    The EFL listening textbook is for advanced learners.

Compare your ideas with those of a classmate or colleague.

The concept of propositions can be used in tasks for testing students' ability to convey meaning while speaking English. For instance, you can give the students the task of finding out what film is playing at a certain theatre, what time it begins, who is starring in it, how long it lasts, and how much the tickets cost. The students can then telephone and leave a voicemail message. Here is an example of what a student might say:

Extract 6

*Uh, hello, Ms. Bailey? This is Julio. The, the movie is Gone with the
Wind. Is star in it Vivien Leigh. I think is Leigh, spell L-E-I-G-H. Is start at
8 o'clock. Is a, uh, a movie of three hours. Uh, is a three-hour movie. I
think is an old movie, not a new movie. Is cost six dollars for one, uh,
one people, I mean, uhm, one person. I think this is all. Bye.*

I have found that this activity works better if you choose an old or
unusual film, rather than something that is currently popular. That way the
students won't be able to rely on frequent radio or television advertisements
to learn the answers to the questions.

Propositional scoring of the students' answers does not deduct points for
grammar errors. Instead, the focus is on whether the learner supplied the
needed information. (Of course, to use a task like this one as an assessment
procedure, you will need to check with the theatre first and make sure that
you know the answers to the questions the learners are trying to answer.)

Action

Score Julio's recording in Extract 6 using propositional scoring. Write the
information he provided on the blank lines below:

What film is playing? _____

What time does it begin? _____

Who is starring in it? _____

How long does it last? _____

How much do the tickets cost? _____

Julio's score = _____ out of five points possible.

8. Conclusion

In this chapter, we have considered the teaching of speaking to beginning
learners and false beginners. After a brief introduction, we looked at some
syllabus design issues in Section 2. Then Section 3 provided a brief discussion
of three important principles that need to be kept in mind when teaching
speaking at this level. Section 4 described and illustrated techniques and
exercise types for introducing and practicing speaking with beginning
students. Section 5 dealt with pronunciation issues. Section 6 provided three
extracts from a lesson where the teacher was focusing on speaking with false
beginner students. Then, Section 7, on assessing learners' speaking, included

some examples of students' speech during a class introduction activity that provides diagnostic information about the students.

The next chapter will cover similar topics, but there we will focus on working with intermediate students. Many of the same procedures can be used at that level, so long as they are adapted appropriately.

Further readings

Bailey, K.M. and L. Savage. 1994. *New Ways in Teaching Speaking.* Alexandria, VA: TESOL.

This book is a collection of short teaching ideas written by teachers for teachers. It includes activities for learners at various levels.

Carter, R. and D. Nunan. 2001. *The Cambridge Guide to Teaching English to Speakers of Other Languages.* Cambridge: Cambridge University Press.

This helpful reference book has short, readable chapters related to many issues discussed here.

Nunan, D. 2004. *Task-based Language Teaching.* Cambridge: Cambridge University Press.

This book provides many ideas for language learning and teaching tasks that can be adapted for different levels of speaking proficiency.

Helpful Web sites

The American Council on the Teaching of Foreign Languages (ACTFL) (www.actfl.org)

The rating guidelines from the American Council on the Teaching of Foreign Languages (ACTFL) are used in Chapters 2, 3, and 4 of this book to describe the speaking of beginning, intermediate, and advanced level learners. Please visit the ACTFL Website (www.actfl.org) for more information.

The Sound Systems of English and Spanish (www.uiowa.edu/~acadtech/phonetics/)

The University of Iowa maintains an excellent Website about the sound systems of English and Spanish. It provides clear demonstrations and explanations of how sounds are produced, including an animated profile of the vocal tract. The Website also produces the phonemes, so learners and teachers can actually hear the various sounds of spoken English.

References

Allen, E.D. and R.M. Valette. 1977. *Classroom Techniques: Foreign Languages and English as a Second Language.* New York, NY: Harcourt Brace Jovanovich, Inc.

American Council on the Teaching of Foreign Languages (ACTFL)

Asher, J.J., J.A. Kusoda, and R. de la Torre. 1993. Learning a Second Language Through Commands: The Second Field Test. In J.W. Oller, Jr. (ed.), *Methods that Work: Ideas for Literacy and Language Teachers (3rd ed.).* Boston: Heinle & Heinle, 13–21.

Bailey, K.M. 1998. *Learning About Language Assessment: Dilemmas, Decisions and Directions.* Boston, MA: Heinle & Heinle.

Bailey, K.M. 2003. Speaking. In D. Nunan (ed.) *Practical English Language Teaching.* New York: McGraw-Hill, 47–66.

Curtis, A. and K.M. Bailey. 2001. Picture Your Students Talking: Using Pictures in the Language Classroom. *ESL Magazine,* July/August: 10–12.

Dell. 2000. *Dell Logic Puzzles.* Norwalk, CT: Dell Magazines, Crosstown Publications.

Freeman, D., Graves, K., and Lee, L. 2005. *ICON Intro International Communication Through English.* New York, NY: McGraw-Hill ESL/ELT

Galvan, J.L., J.A. Pierce, and G.N. Underwood. 1976. The Relevance of Selected Educational Variables of Teachers to their Attitudes Toward Mexican American English. *Journal of the Linguistic Association of the Southwest.* 2: 13–27.

Hammerly, H. 1991. *Fluency and Accuracy: Toward Balance in Language Teaching and Learning.* Clevedon: Multilingual Matters.

Hartmann, P. and L. Blass. 2000. *Quest: Listening and Speaking in the Academic World, Book One.* Boston, MA: McGraw-Hill.

Kozyrev, J.R. 1998. *Talk It Up! Oral Communication for the Real World.* Boston, MA: Houghton Mifflin Company.

Long, M.H., L. Adams, M. McLean, and F. Castaños. 1976. Doing Things with Words–Verbal Interaction in Lockstep and Small Group Classroom Situations. In J.F. Fanselow and R. Crymes (eds.), *On TESOL '76.* Washington, DC: TESOL, 137-153.

Murphy, J. 2003. Pronunciation. In D. Nunan (ed.), *Practical English Language Teaching.* New York, NY: McGraw-Hill, 111–128.

Nunan, D. 2003. *Listen In, Book 1* (2nd ed.). Boston: Thomson Heinle.

Nunan, D. 2005. *Practical English Language Teaching: Grammar.* New York, NY: McGraw-Hill ESL/ELT.

Nunan, D. and C. Lamb. 1996. *The Self-directed Teacher: Managing the Learning Process.* Cambridge: Cambridge University Press.

Pennington, M. 1995. A Situated Process View of Grammar Learning. In M. Pennington (ed.), *New Ways of Teaching Grammar.* Alexandria, VA: TESOL, 135–154.

Skillman, P. and C. McMahill. 1996. *Springboard to Success: Communication Strategies for the Classroom and Beyond.* Upper Saddle River, NJ: Prentice Hall Regents, 30-31.

Stewart, T.W. and C. Vaillette. 2001. *Language Files: Materials for an Introduction to Language and Linguistics* (8th ed.). Columbus: The Ohio State University.

Thrush, E.A., L. Blass, and R. Baldwin. 2002. *Interactions Access: Listening/Speaking* (4th ed.). New York, NY: McGraw-Hill.

Chapter **Three**

Speaking for intermediate level learners

Goals

At the end of this chapter, you should be able to:

 describe the speaking issues that typically concern intermediate learners.

 demonstrate an understanding of confirmation checks, clarification requests, and comprehension checks, and identify instances of each in the speech of intermediate learners.

 demonstrate an understanding of the following key principles to support the teaching of speaking to intermediate learners: negotiation for meaning, developing transactional and interpersonal speech, and personalization.

 create materials and speaking activities for intermediate level learners based on the following task and activity types: information gap and jigsaw activities, role-plays, picture-based activities, and logic puzzles.

 examine pieces of classroom interaction and identify the principles involved in teaching speaking to intermediate learners.

use a diagnostic test to assess learners' pronunciation.

1. Introduction

In this chapter, we will consider techniques for teaching speaking to intermediate learners. These descriptors from the ACTFL guidelines list the characteristics of intermediate students' speaking ability. You might wish to contrast these statements with those about beginning students (see Chapter 2). Intermediate level learners are able to:

- handle successfully a variety of uncomplicated, basic and communicative tasks and social situations;
- talk simply about self and family members;
- ask and answer questions and participate in simple conversations on topics beyond the most immediate needs, e.g. personal history and leisure time activities;
- increase utterance length slightly, but speech may continue to be characterized by frequent long pauses, since the smooth incorporation of even basic conversational strategies is often hindered;
- improve pronunciation, which may continue to be strongly influenced by first language, and fluency may still be strained.

The ACTFL guidelines note the important role of the listener, when they state that although misunderstandings still arise, speakers at the intermediate level can usually be understood by sympathetic interlocutors.

Reflection

Think about a non-native speaker whom you consider to be an intermediate learner of English. What are the characteristics of that person's speech that make you think of him as "intermediate"?

Talk to three intermediate learners of English. According to these learners, what are their main goals for studying English? Focus specifically on spoken English. What are their current strengths? What areas do they most want to improve upon next? Now think about your own assessment of these people's speaking skills? What do you think are their current strengths in speaking English? What areas should they work to improve first? Fill out the chart below:

Which person	His/Her ideas	Your ideas
Learner #1		
Learner #2		
Learner #3		

Where your ideas differ from the learners', what accounts for the differences?

We will turn now to a brief discussion of issues that influence syllabus design. Next we will consider three important principles as well as tasks and materials for teaching speaking at the intermediate level. Then we will look at teaching pronunciation for intermediate learners before examining some classroom extracts. Finally, we will think about assessing intermediate students' speaking skills, focusing especially on pronunciation.

2. Syllabus design issues

At the intermediate level, syllabus design issues become very diverse, since these learners already know a great deal of English, but still need to know more. As the teacher you will need to help your intermediate students build their vocabularies, improve their grammar, and extend the range of speech acts they can use appropriately. (See page 5 to review these concepts.) They may also need to improve their pronunciation accuracy. In addition, while you and the learners are expanding their communicative competence, you can do a great deal to increase their communicative confidence.

Review the table of contents or the Scope and Sequence of three intermediate-level speaking textbooks. How are they organized—by topical themes, by functions, or by grammar points (or perhaps by some combination of these ways)? Sometimes you can view the table of contents of a book online, in case you can't find the book itself.

Some course books cover both listening and speaking, which is sensible since these two aural/oral skills often work together. For instance, as shown in Example 1, in Kozyrev's (1998) book, *Talk It Up!*, every chapter has three listening activities, some pronunciation work, and suggestions for groupwork. The chapters are organized around themes, such as Friends, Feeling at Home, Making Connections, The World of Work, Money Matters, and so on. These topics provide relevant vocabulary, grammar structures, and examples of speech acts, as well as something to talk about.

Example 1

Talk It Up! Oral Communication for the Real World (Kozyrev, 1998, p. iii-iv)

Some syllabuses and methods are designed to emphasize input to the learners, while others emphasize interaction. What is the difference? **Input** is "language which a learner hears or receives and from which he or she can learn" (Richards, Platt and Weber, 1985, p. 143). Input can be unidirectional. That is, learners can gain input just by reading or listening, without responding in any way. That subset of the input which learners notice, find helpful, and learn from is called **intake.** Not all the input to learners can be converted to intake. For instance, speech that is too fast for learners to process will not become intake.

In contrast, **interaction** is, by definition, not unidirectional. Interactive speech involves at least two people communicating with one another. During verbal interaction, people exchange information and ideas (Long, 1983) and communicate their needs. During these conversations there are opportunities for "the less competent speaker to provide feedback on his or her lack of understanding" (p. 214). In the process, most (sympathetic) interlocutors will adjust their speech to help the learner understand better. The result is what

Long calls the "negotiated modification of the conversation" (ibid.). This negotiation for meaning makes the input to the learner comprehensible, meaning that it is understood and can be converted to intake. It is hypothesized that language acquisition occurs as a result of these processes.

One benefit of learners interacting in English is that when we speak (or write) in a new language, we have to focus on our grammatical accuracy and on our pronunciation in order to be understood. It appears that in trying to speak, learners have many opportunities to notice the gap between their **output** (their own speech or writing in the target language) and that of native or more proficient users of English (see Swain, 1995).

In the early days of second language acquisition research, some people thought that **comprehensible input** addressed to the language learner was what caused language acquisition to occur (see Krashen, 1985). More recently, researchers have studied interaction. They have identified several important processes that help people convert input to intake through the negotiation for meaning that occurs during the interaction. Pica, Young, and Doughty (1987, p. 740) have provided the following definitions of processes that occur as learners converse in their new language:

- **Clarification request:** ...One speaker seeks assistance in understanding the other speaker's preceding utterance through questions..., statements such as *I don't understand,* or imperatives such as *Please repeat.*
- **Comprehension check:** ...One speaker attempts to determine whether the other speaker has understood a preceding message.
- **Confirmation check:** ...One speaker seeks confirmation of the other's preceding utterance through repetition, with rising intonation, of what was perceived to be all or part of the preceding utterance.

Below are some examples of clarification requests, comprehension checks, and confirmation checks. These categories can be a little confusing because of the changing roles of the persons who are the "speaker" and the "interlocutor(s)." The key difference between the comprehension check and the confirmation check is that the comprehension check is the speaker checking *someone else's* understanding, while in the confirmation check a person is checking *his/her* own understanding of what the other speaker has said. This distinction can be a little confusing because the person who is the designated speaker changes as the turns of a conversation alternate, as we see in the following extract:

John, a male ESL teacher in California, is interviewing Kim, a newly arrived female ESL student from Korea. The following (totally constructed) conversation occurs:

John: *So tell me a little bit about yourself.*

Kim: *Uh, so, you mean, uh, my life?* **(CLARIFICATION REQUEST)**

John: *Yeah, like where're you from, whaddya like to do, and stuff like that.*

Kim: *Uh, I'm Christian. I born Seoul.*

John: *Uhm, you were born with a soul? Like from Heaven?* **(CLARIFICATION REQUEST**, *John asking Kim to clarify her previous utterance.***)**

Kim: *Oh! No. Seoul. My city, uh, in my country. I from Korea.*

John: *Oh! You were born in Seoul, Korea. Is that it?* **(CONFIRMATION CHECK**, *John—as the speaker—is confirming his understanding of Kim's previous comment. Here Kim is the interlocutor for the moment.***)**

Kim: *Yes. Seoul is capital of my country. Korea my country. I born Seoul. You understand me?* **(COMPREHENSION CHECK**, *where Kim is the speaker and she is checking John's understanding.***)**

You can see that as the conversation goes on, John and Kim negotiate for meaning by checking with each other, asking questions, and seeking clarification. The continuation of their conversation is in the Action box below.

Action

In each blank below, indicate whether the preceding utterance is a confirmation check, a comprehension check, or a clarification request.

John: Yes, you were born in Seoul, in Korea. And you said you are a Christian? _____ (Hint: John is making sure he understands what Kim was saying earlier.)

Kim: Yes. Baptist. Is many Baptist church.

John: Oh, you mean in Seoul? There are many Baptist churches in Seoul? _____ (Hint: John—as the speaker for a moment—is making sure he has understood Kim's meaning.)

Kim: Yeah. And all Korea.

John: All Korea? _____ (Hint: John is asking for more information from Kim about her immediately preceding statement.)

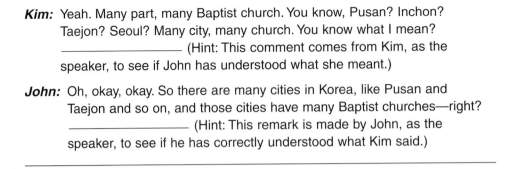

Kim: Yeah. Many part, many Baptist church. You know, Pusan? Inchon? Taejon? Seoul? Many city, many church. You know what I mean?
_____ (Hint: This comment comes from Kim, as the speaker, to see if John has understood what she meant.)

John: Oh, okay, okay. So there are many cities in Korea, like Pusan and Taejon and so on, and those cities have many Baptist churches—right?
_____ (Hint: This remark is made by John, as the speaker, to see if he has correctly understood what Kim said.)

Your textbook and/or syllabus for teaching speaking may be organized around grammar points, topical themes, or speech acts. Often different chapters of textbooks use themes (such as "Family Ties" or "Travel Experiences") to introduce, or "carry," lessons on grammar points, vocabulary items, speech acts, and so on. (As a result, these themes are sometimes referred to as "carrier topics.") Regardless of the syllabus or textbook structure, it is important for you as the teacher to encourage your intermediate learners to interact in English because interaction seems to promote language acquisition. We turn now to a discussion of three important principles to follow when teaching speaking to intermediate learners.

3. Principles for teaching speaking to intermediate learners

All of the principles in this book are useful, to varying degrees, across all proficiency levels. However, in this section we consider those principles that are most relevant to teaching speaking to intermediate students. For this reason, the following three principles are discussed:

- Plan speaking tasks that involve negotiation for meaning.
- Design both transactional and interpersonal speaking activities.
- Personalize the speaking activities whenever possible.

1. Plan speaking tasks that involve negotiation for meaning.

It appears that in the process of negotiating for meaning, the language addressed to learners gets adjusted to their level and becomes comprehensible to them. And as learners work to make themselves understood (either in speech or in writing), they must attend to accuracy. That is, they must select the right vocabulary, apply grammar rules, pronounce words carefully, and so on. In doing so, they may "notice the gap" (Schmidt and Frota, 1986, pp. 310–315) between what they want to say and what they can say, or between what they say and what other people say. By planning speaking tasks that require learners to negotiate for meaning, teachers can give students valuable chances for practice and language development.

For students at the intermediate level, information gap and jigsaw activities can provide many opportunities for learners to negotiate for meaning. This is especially true if the pairwork or groupwork is supposed to lead to a conclusion or solution. (We will examine an example in Section 6 on page 109, when we consider speaking in the intermediate classroom.)

2. Design both transactional and interpersonal speaking activities.

When we talk with someone outside the classroom, we usually do so for interpersonal or transactional purposes. What do these terms mean? **Interpersonal speech** is communication for social purposes, including establishing and maintaining social relationships. **Transactional speech** involves communicating to get something done, such as the exchange of goods and/or services.

Most spoken interactions "can be placed on a continuum from relatively predictable to relatively unpredictable" (Nunan, 1991, p. 42). Casual conversations—an example of interpersonal speech—are relatively unpredictable and can range over many topics, with the participants taking turns and commenting freely. In contrast, Nunan says that "transactional encounters of a fairly restricted kind will usually contain highly predictable patterns" (1991, p. 42), and he gives the example of telephoning for a taxi. In contrast, interactional speech is more fluid and unpredictable. Our students will need to use English in both transactional and interactional settings, so it is important that classroom speaking activities embody both purposes.

3. Personalize the content of speaking activities whenever possible.

Some very early language classroom research revealed that personalization is important. **Personalization** is the process of making activities match the learners' own circumstances, interests, and goals. Omaggio (1982) showed that teachers who personalized language lessons were judged to be effective, by both their supervisors and their students.

Personalizing an exercise can be as simple as using students' names, academic majors, cities, or jobs in speaking activities. Or you can build role-plays around situations suggested by the learners. You can also use song lyrics or reading passages selected by the students or based on their interests as the basis of logic puzzles and picture-based activities. Personalizing language lessons is partly a matter of careful planning and partly of responding creatively to students' questions and comments during activities. (See Nunan, 2005, for a discussion of personalizing grammar lessons.)

4. Tasks and materials

As in Chapter 2, this section is meant to illustrate some key task and exercise types for teaching speaking, but here we will focus on intermediate learners. The exercise types we will consider are as follows:

1. Role-plays
2. Picture-based activities
3. Logic puzzles
4. Information gap and jigsaw activities

Review the table of contents of three ESL/EFL speaking textbooks aimed at intermediate level learners, and make an inventory of the activities that are common to them. What are the five most frequently occurring activities for practicing speaking? Are they based on themes, vocabulary items, speech acts, or grammatical structures in some way? Choose an activity that appeals to you and try it out with your own English students, or with a few willing peers if you aren't teaching yet.

1. Role-plays

In a lesson on communication strategies I used with my intermediate EFL learners in Hong Kong, I wanted to set up a context that would create a need for my students to use communication strategies. So I gave them the following task for a role-play about a shopping trip: "Your grandmother sends you to the corner store with a list of things she needs. But when you get to the store, the shopkeeper is not there. Instead, an American woman is tending the store, and she doesn't speak Cantonese. Unfortunately, you do not see some of the things your grandmother sent you to buy. So even though you know the Cantonese names of the items your grandmother wants, you must explain them to the woman in English."

Think about the English learners you work with (or plan to work with). How could you modify the activity described above to fit better with their circumstances and goals? (For instance, my young Hong Kong students were likely to be sent to the store by their grandmothers, but that may not be the case if you are working with oil company managers in Kyrgyzstan.)

To set up this activity, follow these steps:

1. Bring in to class small, household items that your intermediate students are not likely to know the English names for, such as fingernail clippers, corkscrews, potato peelers, safety pins, staple removers, coasters, emery boards, battery testers, and so on.

2. You should also bring some "dummy" items that are similar to but not exactly what the students are supposed to describe.

3. Bring two of each item and divide the items into two matching sets. Hide one set in the teacher's desk drawer along with several other objects. This is the "shop" from which the "shopkeeper" will try to choose the described object. Then conceal the items of the second set in individual opaque plastic bags. The individual objects hidden in the bags give the students clear visual representations of the things they must describe.

4. Show the item in one plastic bag to a student. This is the thing he must buy, but since he doesn't know its name, he must describe the object to the "shopkeeper" in English.

Action

Make a list of six or eight additional items that could be used in the shopping trip activity to encourage students to use communication strategies when they don't know the name of an item or a particular verb to describe a process. Pool your list with those of your colleagues or classmates. (Items should be familiar objects that are common enough that students could imagine buying them, but not so well known that intermediate students will know their names in English. The objects should also be unbreakable, cheap, and small enough for you to transport them easily to your classroom.)

The point of this exercise is not for students to learn the names of obscure household items (although they usually like the vocabulary element of the activity and typically write down the new words they learn in the process).

Instead, the purpose is to create a context in which students must practice using communication strategies. More importantly, the activity lets them do so in a safe atmosphere with a supportive person who does not speak (or pretends not to speak) the students' first language, so they cannot resort to using the name of the object in their native tongue. (We will revisit this role-play later in the chapter when we examine how one intermediate learner carried out this task.)

Role-plays are the ideal vehicle for practicing speech acts with intermediate learners. Role-plays allow students to try out appropriate English utterances in potentially difficult situations, before they must use them in real life. For example, it is important to be able to apologize appropriately if we hurt or offend someone. The social rules for when and how to apologize (and how often) vary from one culture to another so for learners to simply translate expressions from their mother tongues into English may not work too well.

In addition, how we apologize is partly governed by the formality of the situation and our familiarity with the person we have hurt or offended. When you design a role-play for practicing English apologies, you can set up simple role cards—one for the person who apologizes and one for the person who responds. For example, here is some guidance about apologizing for intermediate learners from a widely used textbook:

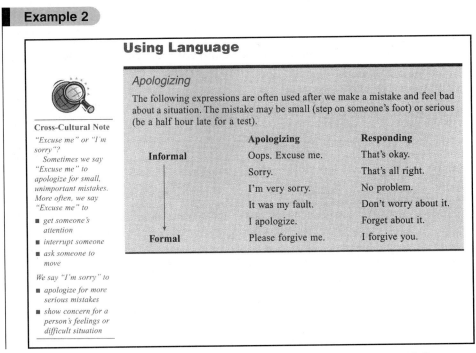

Example 2

Using Language

Apologizing

The following expressions are often used after we make a mistake and feel bad about a situation. The mistake may be small (step on someone's foot) or serious (be a half hour late for a test).

Cross-Cultural Note

"Excuse me" or "I'm sorry"?
Sometimes we say "Excuse me" to apologize for small, unimportant mistakes. More often, we say "Excuse me" to

- *get someone's attention*
- *interrupt someone*
- *ask someone to move*

We say "I'm sorry" to

- *apologize for more serious mistakes*
- *show concern for a person's feelings or difficult situation*

	Apologizing	Responding
Informal	Oops. Excuse me.	That's okay.
	Sorry.	That's all right.
	I'm very sorry.	No problem.
	It was my fault.	Don't worry about it.
	I apologize.	Forget about it.
Formal	Please forgive me.	I forgive you.

Interactions 1: Listening/Speaking (Tanka, Most, and Baker, 2002, p. 104)

How we apologize and respond to apologies is shaped by the situation. In teaching and practicing apologies with your students, be sure to vary the context and the age and status of the participants. For instance, have students apologize after bumping into an elderly lady, a five-year-old boy, a well-dressed business person, and so on.

Another difficult context for English learners is using speech acts that may disappoint, hurt, or offend their interlocutors. One such situation is refusing invitations. Here is a set-up from the same textbook in which the invitation is provided and the learners must give the response to the invitation.

Example 3

8 **Refusing Invitations.** With a partner, take turns inviting and refusing the following invitations. To be polite, you should try to explain why you can't accept. You might suggest getting together another time. Here are some more ways to refuse an invitation:

Thanks, but I can't. I have to work.
Thanks for asking, but I have other plans.
I'd love to, but I'm busy. Maybe some other time.

1. *A:* Would you like to go swimming this afternoon?
   B: _____

2. *A:* Why don't you have a cup of coffee with us?
   B: _____

3. *A:* Do you want to go to the ball game tomorrow? I have an extra ticket.
   B: _____

4. *A:* We're going dancing Saturday night. Would you like to come?
   B: _____

Interactions 1: Listening/Speaking (Tanka, Most, and Baker 2002, p. 173)

After this kind of practice, students can engage in role-plays in which they think up their own invitations and refusals. To make the speech act more challenging, you can remove the non-verbal element of face-to-face communication and have students make and decline invitations on the telephone. For example, one student can call another (perhaps at a pre-arranged time), and invite him to go to a movie. The other student knows he must decline politely. Later the class can discuss what worked and what was challenging about the experience.

The exercise in Example 2 (p. 100) uses interpersonal speech. Think of the students you teach (or would like to teach). How could you change the four questions in Example 3 so that they involve personalization?

Transactional speech often occurs between people who don't know one another personally. So although transactional speech is predictable (in terms of the vocabulary, grammar, and speech acts involved), it is also risky. In English speaking lessons, teachers can help learners prepare for taking risks. Classroom role-plays, followed by supportive feedback, can help intermediate learners prepare for transactional speaking in English.

Sometimes role cards are used to give students guidance about what to say in a role-play. Here is an example of four different roles that could be used in a role-play for practicing transactional speech. The learners participate in a role-play about ordering dinner in a restaurant setting:

Example 4

Waiter:	You never know what to recommend.
Customer 1:	You're on a diet.
Customer 2:	You're a vegetarian.
Customer 3:	You're on a budget.

All three customers can't make up their minds.

Use this menu. After practicing, show the class. Can you guess which customer is which?

RON'S KITCHEN

SOUP			COFFEE AND TEA			PASTA	
POTATO LEEK IN A CUP	1.95					SPAGHETTI BOLOGNESE	8.95
TUSCAN BEAN SOUP	3.95		COFFEE	1.25		EGGPLANT LASAGNA	7.95
ITALIAN TOMATO	3.95		SINGLE ESPRESSO	1.75		CHICKEN FETTUCCINE	8.95
			DOUBLE ESPRESSO	3.25			
SALAD			CAPPUCCINO	2.50		DESSERTS	
RON'S MIXED LEAF	6.95		SPECIALITY TEAS	1.25		RON'S RUM BABA	3.95
ORIENTAL CHICKEN	9.50		(EARL GREY, CHAMOMILLE)			TIRAMISU	4.95
SHRIMP RONNIE	8.95		HOT CHOCOLATE	2.00		HOT FUDGE SUNDAE	4.50
						FRUIT SORBET	3.50
PIZZA						LEMON CHEESECAKE	4.50
SANTA FE CHICKEN	9.95					DEATH BY CHOCOLATE	5.50
PEKING DUCK	10.95					APPLE PIE	2.50
THREE SAUSAGE	8.50						

Conversation Lessons: The Natural Language of Conversations
(An Intermediate Course) (Martinez, 1997, p. 15)

Doing a role-play well demands that students use their linguistic, sociolinguistic, and discourse competence, and sometimes their strategic competence. It may help your learners to do role-plays like this if they can first hear some recordings of other people doing the same task. It can also be helpful to practice some standard phrases first. Here is a textbook exercise that has learners identify whether utterances were said by a store clerk or a customer.

Example 5

> ### 3 Who said it?
>
> **Some things below were said by a customer and the others by a shopkeeper. Decide who said what.**
>
> 1. I'll be right with you. _____
> 2. How are you today? _____
> 3. Would you like to try that on? _____
> 4. Do you have it in a larger size? _____
> 5. Thanks for waiting. _____
> 6. What time do you close? _____
> 7. We're out of that size. _____
> 8. It's on sale. _____
> 9. I can order it for you if you like. _____
> 10. Will that be cash or credit card? _____
> 11. Do you carry men's shoes? _____
> 12. What's your return policy? _____
> 13. Would you like a receipt? _____
> 14. Will that be all for you today? _____
> 15. I'd appreciate that. _____
>
> **Now work out a new dialogue using all the phrases in this unit.**

Conversation Lessons: The Natural Language of Conversations (An Intermediate Course) (Martinez, 1997, p. 115)

You can also personalize this kind of textbook task by bringing photocopies of an actual menu from a restaurant in your city, which the students would like to visit in the future. (If the menu is printed in a language other than English you will need to translate the items into English.) If you are working with adult or secondary school students, in some cultures you might actually be able to go to the restaurant for a class party.

Ask two different pairs of native speakers or proficient English users to carry out these role-plays. Record the role-plays and listen to the interactions. Did the speakers use the language you predicted? Did they use other language? How would you modify your procedures in light of this information?

Carrying out transactional speech on the telephone can be very challenging for intermediate learners. Telephone communication lacks the physical context and support of nonverbal behavior that learners can rely on in face-to-face interactions. Example 6 is a role-play set-up based on transactional speech on the telephone.

Situation 1: Dentist's office
Roles: patient and receptionist

Patient's Instructions
1. Call the dentist's office to change your appointment. Tell the receptionist:
   a. the time of your old appointment
   b. the reason for the change
2. Arrange a new appointment time with the receptionist.

Receptionist's Instructions
1. A patient will call you to make an appointment. Answer the phone politely, then listen to the patient's problem.
2. Arrange a new appointment time with the patient.

Adapted from Tanka, Most, & Baker, 2002, p. 126

2. Picture-based activities: Collaborative story telling

Intermediate learners have many strengths in terms of the grammar and vocabulary they already know. You can design activities in which their **receptive vocabulary** can become **productive vocabulary** through discussion and use. One of my favorite picture-based activities gives students speaking opportunities at the same time it helps activate expressive vocabulary.

This is a story construction activity. It can be done individually or in pairs or groups. I like working with small groups to do this task, since the students can scaffold one another's learning and build on each other's ideas. For this activity you need a collection of mounted or laminated photographs from magazines or calendars. The use of high-interest photographs draws on a principle introduced in Chapter 2: Provide something for people to talk about.

Good choices of photos for prompting collaborative story telling include the following:

1. A leading lady (someone intriguing looking)
2. A leading man (again, an intriguing or interesting looking person)
3. Someone sinister or mysterious (either a man or a woman will do)
4. Something valuable (jewels, a crown, a bar of gold, a bag of money)

5. A dangerous looking place (a cliff edge, a mountain top, the top of a tall building, the edge of a volcano, sand dunes in a desert scene)

6. Some form of transportation (a plane, a speedboat, a canoe, a sports car)

Six photographs provide enough material for a group of three students to build a story with a sentence or two about each picture. Students work together in small groups to determine the sequence and the plot of the story suggested by the pictures. Then, when they are ready, each group recites its story, holding up the individual pictures as the story proceeds. I have used this activity with many different sets of similar pictures, and the groups have come up with surprisingly creative and diverse stories.

If you have a big class or a more advanced group, additional pictures can be used to make the stories more complex. For instance, you can add a picture of some kind of beverage (a canteen of water, a bottle of whiskey, fresh-squeezed orange juice, a sports drink, two glasses of champagne), or a threatening animal (a coiled snake, a crouching lion, a snarling dog, a charging bull), or a dangerous object (a dagger, a musket, poison, a hangman's noose, a lighted match).

The group's pictures don't need to be identical, but they should be parallel in content and each group should have the same number of pictures. After every group has told its story (holding up the appropriate pictures as illustrations while the story unfolds), the class can vote on the best story.

Turn through the pages of several magazines to find several large, colorful photographs that would interest your students or future students. (You can also locate downloadable photographs on the Internet.) Write the instructions to the learners for a collaborative story telling activity using the pictures you find.

3. Logic puzzles as the basis for speaking activities

Here is another logic puzzle (adapted from *Dell Logic Puzzles,* 2000). You will notice that this one has fewer clues than the puzzle in Chapter 2, and that the clues are longer and more complex linguistically. (They involve past tense, comparatives and superlatives, and more unusual vocabulary.) Once again, the puzzle can be used as it is for groupwork, or it can be turned into a jigsaw activity in which two students are given different but complementary sets of information, which they must then share in English in order to solve the puzzle. Here's the situation, set up as a worksheet to be given to the students:

Example 7

Logic Puzzle Worksheet   Name: _____

Five students eat lunch at the school cafeteria. One after another, the five students each ordered a different meal. From the following clues, try to determine the order in which the children came into the cafeteria, what each one ate, and how old each child is.

Clue #1: The twelve-year-old ate before the student who ordered the sushi but after Cathy.

Clue #2: The friend who ate pasta is a year older than the first child but younger than Reggie.

Clue #3: The last student is a year younger than the one who ate a hamburger but older than Juan.

Clue #4: The student who ate the shish-kabob was one of the last two to buy lunch. This person is younger than Kumi but older than the third student.

Clue #5: The eight-year-old ordered immediately before the one who had pasta and immediately after Reggie.

Clue #6: The children are aged from eight to twelve and no two students are the same age.

Clue #7: One person ordered tacos for lunch.

Clue #8: One person was named Malaika.

Directions: Use this chart to record the facts you know from the clues. Put an "X" where the facts do <u>NOT</u> match. Put an "O" where the facts <u>DO</u> match. A blank cell means you still have to figure out about that clue.

Here is the key to the labels in the chart. The single initials stand for the children's names (Cathy, Juan, Kumi, Malaika, and Reggie). The cardinal numbers represent their ages (8, 9, 10, 11, and 12). The two letters together represent the various foods (hamburger, shish-kabob, tacos, sushi, and pasta). The ordinal numbers (1st, 2nd, 3rd, 4th, 5th) represent the sequence in which they bought their lunches.

	C	J	K	M	R	8	9	10	11	12	Hb	Sh	Ta	Su	Pa
1st															
2nd															
3rd															
4th															
5th															
Hb															
Sh															
Ta															
Su															
Pa															
8															
9															
10															
11															
12															

Reflection

How would intermediate students react to this puzzle? How long do you think it would take them to solve it? What vocabulary, if any, would you want to pre-teach?

Students can use the clues and the chart on the worksheet to eliminate impossible connections (with an X in the cell). They can add an O in the cell where they have found a sure match. A blank cell means a conclusion about this possible combination has not yet been reached.

This activity can go on for some time. At some point you should have the students switch their groups, or compare their logic across groups, in order to pool their information and coach one another. You can also have a whole class check-in after about fifteen minutes, to see if the entire group agrees on the statements they know to be true. (This step can easily be done if you make a photocopied overhead transparency of the grid above and mark on it with washable ink pens.) My advice for you is not to have your students attempt a puzzle like this until you yourself have done it. Be prepared to give guidance and hints, and also to let the students take the puzzle home to work on it. Plan some time to revisit the puzzle in the next class if you do, so the students can come to closure. (The solution is printed on page 118 at the end of this chapter.)

Action

Try working this puzzle with a friend and tape record your interaction. What kinds of language (vocabulary, grammatical structures, speech acts) do you use as you try to do the puzzle? How long does it take you to solve it?

Now, using the example in Chapter 2 (page 56) as a model, divide the clues above to create a jigsaw activity for pairs of students.

Reflection

Fotos (1995, pp. 181–182) argues that the most communication is produced among students if speaking tasks have four components: (1) they contain an information gap, (2) students are given time to plan what they are going to say, (3) the tasks require a solution, and (4) all students must reach agreement on the solution. Which of these four components listed above are present in the logic puzzle about the children having lunch in the cafeteria?

This Reflection box and Fotos's point about four key components reveal why logic puzzles and similar activities are such powerful communication tasks. The participants must use the available information to sort out the solution. Doing so in English provides ample opportunity for intermediate students to negotiate for meaning.

Reflection

Predict the sorts of language that your students will need to solve the information gap task you designed based on this logic puzzle. That is, what sorts of grammatical structures, vocabulary items, and speech acts do you think students will need to use in order to collaborate and solve the puzzle? What concepts and vocabulary might you want to pre-teach before having your class of intermediate learners try this task?

This puzzle framework can be adapted and personalized for use with many different kinds of students. For instance, a puzzle about eight to twelve-year-old children eating lunch in a cafeteria may not be appropriate for the Japanese businessmen you teach in Tokyo. You can use the clues above to generate an appropriate puzzle by changing the food ordering sequence to the order in which the men boarded the train at Tokyo Station, changing the names (to Mr. Seiko, Mr. Komatsu, Mr. Igawa, Mr. Kato, and Mr. Akamatsu), and changing the types of foods to professions (accountant, banker, marketing manager, chief salesman, advertising executive). Or if you are teaching secondary school students in Latin America, you can use students' first names, list the sequence in which they enter the classroom, give their birthdates, and identify their favorite sports. The basic puzzle framework can be manipulated in many different ways to create several challenging communicative activities for speaking English.

Action

Using the logic puzzle above as the basic framework, change the contents to create a puzzle that is age-appropriate for your students, or your future students, and that represents their interests.

Try to solve the new version of the puzzle with a friend before you have your students attempt it. Time yourselves so you'll have an idea of how long the task will take during the lesson.

Teachers often have to decide, when using a communication activity, whether to pre-teach vocabulary and structures or wait and see what the students can manage on their own. With intermediate learners, it's sometimes best to let them attempt a task and see what they already know. That way you can respond to their questions as needed, instead of covering material they've already learned. Responding is more efficient and motivating, while teaching something the students already know is time-consuming and demotivating.

5. Teaching pronunciation

At the intermediate level, English learners are able to accomplish many goals by speaking. They are also typically becoming more sensitive to the input available to them than they were as lower-level students. As a result, they notice variations in the spoken language that they hear. They may also be willing to take risks to try to sound more natural while speaking English.

Your intermediate students may want to learn about pronunciation differences across varieties of spoken English. Although you may be more familiar with one variety than another, you can use audio or video recordings, guest speakers, information from the Internet, and published materials to help your learners become aware of pronunciation differences. For example, here is an excerpt from an intermediate textbook, which contrasts British and American English pronunciation:

Example 8

Pronunciation

The American /t/

In some words, speakers of American English pronounce /t/ between two vowels as a quick /d/ sound. You can hear this sound frequently when we say "it" after /t/:

Get it.   Take it off.   Fill it in.   Put it out right away.

This pronunciation change does not happen in British English.

Contrast: American English: "better" /beder/
British English: "better" /beter/

Interactions 1: Listening/Speaking (Tanka, Most, and Baker, 2002, pp. 183–184)

6. Speaking in the intermediate classroom

In this section, we look at an extended example of language produced in a role-play in an intermediate level classroom. The exchange involves the transactional speech needed to do the shopping trip role-play task described on pages 98-99. You will see that although the student involved has some gaps in his English vocabulary, and his grammar isn't perfect, he is still able to say a great deal and get his point across.

In a sense, this role-play involves a "reverse information gap." In a regular information gap activity, one person has information that another lacks, and he or she must use English to convey that information. This kind of activity adds a new twist to the usual information gap task, because the "gap" here is a linguistic one. In this activity, the speaker (a language learner) must "buy" something from another person, and although he knows what he must buy, he doesn't know the name of that object in English. So in order to convey the information about his needs to the "seller" of the object, the learner must use communication strategies to get his point across.

Reflection

Think about the shopping activity for practicing communication strategies. What kinds of communication strategies would you use if you were trying to buy something in another country and you didn't know the name of the item in that country's language?

Here is a role-play conversation that occurred between one of my Hong Kong students (S for student) and me (T for teacher), when the student found a monolingual English speaker instead of the familiar Cantonese-speaking clerk at a neighborhood store. The student was trying to "buy" round cork coasters without knowing the word for *coaster*. All of my "props" were hidden on the shelf of a podium, so they were available to me, but not visible to the class.

Extract 2

S: *Uh, hello. Where is Mr. Lim?*

T: *Mr. Lim isn't here today. May I help you?* (smiling expectantly)

S: *Uh, I must buy something—uh—*(laughs). *My grandmother said to buy something.*

Ss: (Laughter from his classmates as he glances around the room)

T: *What do you need to buy?* (said with an encouraging tone)

S: *Uh, I dunno know how to say this thing. I don't know the name.*

T: *Okay, what is it for?*

S: *Uh, okay, okay, it is for drinking.*

T: *Oh, how about this?* (pulls out a canned soft drink from behind the barrier)

S: *Oh, no!* (surprised tone)

Ss: (More laughter from his classmates)

S: *It's for having a drink—it's not the thing to drink.*

T: Oh, okay! Here you go! (pulls out a plastic drinking glass from the podium shelf)

Ss: (More laughter from the class)

S: Oh, no! It's not this. Is, uh, how you say (turns to the class, asks them a question in Cantonese; they laugh and the teacher smiles and waits)—oh! It is going under the drink. We put it under the drink so no water on the table (gesturing by sliding one hand under the other).

T: Oh, I understand! (looks hopeful and pulls out a paper napkin)

S: Oh, no! (His classmates laugh uproariously)

T: This goes under the drink to keep the table from getting wet. Isn't this right? (looking hopeful)

S: (Laughing and shaking his head) No, not this thing.

T: Oh! (sounds disappointed and looks crestfallen)

S: (Turns and speaks to his classmates in Cantonese)

Ss: Cork, cork!

S: It is cork. This thing is cork.

T: Oh, cork! Okay, here it is! (looking pleased, pulls out a single cork which has been removed from a bottle)

Ss: (More loud laughter and some coaching in English and Cantonese)

Reflection

At the beginning of this chapter on pages 96–98, we considered three principles for teaching speaking to intermediate learners. These involved (1) negotiation for meaning, (2) transactional and interpersonal speech, and (3) personalization of language exercises. Is each of these principles illustrated in Extract 2 above? If so, how? Underline or highlight examples of these principles in Extract 2.

As the role-play activity continues the student uses more communication strategies to get his point across. I was pleased at his effort, since this was the point of the lesson. Here is how the interaction ended:

Extract 3

S: Oh, okay, no (laughing). It's not this thing. It's, uhm, okay—it's, uhm, for under the drink so no water on the table. But is flat. Not paper. Is cork. Is flat cork for under, eh, the drink. Is like this (making a round shape about three inches in diameter with the thumb and forefingers of both hands).

T: Oh! I understand! You want to buy coasters! (pulling out a round cork coaster from the bag of hidden items)

S: (Obviously relieved and pleased) *Yes! Yes! This is the thing!* (His classmates laugh and applaud his effort.) *What is the name?*

T: What is it called? Coaster. We call these coasters.

S: How to spell it please?

T: How is it spelled? C-O-A-S-T-E-R-S.

S: Can you write it please? (gesturing to the whiteboard)

T: (Gives him the whiteboard marker) *I'll spell it and you write it for the class, okay? C-O-A-S-T-E-R-S.*

S: Oh, okay, okay. Coasters. (He prints the word on the whiteboard as the teacher spells it aloud.) *Coasters* (holding up the coaster triumphantly to show his classmates). *This is a coaster!* (announced dramatically)

Ss: Coasters, coasters! (Prolonged applause as the student resumes his seat)

Reflection

In Extracts 1 and 2, the teacher is trying to get the student to use communication strategies. Do you think that the shopping task is effective for this purpose? Why or why not?

Underline or highlight all the communication strategies used by the student in Extracts 1 and 2. Compare your ideas to those of a classmate or colleague.

7. Assessing intermediate learners

Assessing intermediate students' speaking skills is very important. By definition, intermediate students have already accomplished a great deal in their learning of English, but likewise, they still have more to learn. Therefore, it is vital that any assessment procedures we may use are reliable and valid, and that they provide us teachers, as well as our students, with useful information for making decisions.

Assessing the pronunciation of intermediate students is also important. At this level, learners can typically make most of their needs understood and will be able to engage in a wide range of communicative activities, using

English with both native and non-native speakers to express their ideas, get their needs met, and convey emotions. It is important to help them improve their pronunciation to the point where they can be easily understood by most of the people with whom they will speak English.

Once when a friend of mine was teaching English at the university level in England, she was surprised when a group of her Chinese engineering students (all males) asked her where they could go in England to buy "cotton petticoats." After some negotiation, she realized that what they were really hoping to find was "cotton padded coats." This example illustrates that even very small pronunciation errors can create miscommunications.

The "Prator Passage" is a diagnostic test, which was designed to identify areas for improvement in university students' production of the English segmental and suprasegmental phonemes. The Prator Passage (Prator and Robinett, 1985, pp. 236–237) is reproduced below:

THE PRATOR DIAGNOSTIC PASSAGE

(1) When a student from another country comes to study in the United States, he has to find the answers to many questions, and he has many problems to think about. (2) Where should he live? (3) Would it be better if he looked for a private room off campus or if he stayed in a dormitory? (4) Should he spend all of his time just studying? (5) Shouldn't he try to take advantage of the many social and cultural activities which are offered? (6) At first it is not easy for him to be casual in dress, informal in manner, and confident in speech. (7) Little by little he learns what kind of clothing is usually worn here to be casually dressed for classes. (8) He also learns to choose the language and customs, which are appropriate for informal situations. (9) Finally he begins to feel sure of himself. (10) But let me tell you, my friend, this long-awaited feeling doesn't develop suddenly—does it? (11) All of this takes will power.

Action

The Prator Passage contains the segmental phonemes of North American English. Check the text against the vowel and consonant charts on pages 65 and 68, to make sure it contains at least two instances of every vowel and consonant sound.

The Prator Passage was also designed to elicit some important suprasegmental phonemes of English (p. 13). For instance, the various question types included in the paragraph call for different intonation contours.

Action

Consider sentences 2, 3, 4, 5, 6, and 10 from the Prator Passage. What intonation pattern is each one intended to assess? Read each line aloud and listen to your own voice.

Now ask a colleague or classmate who is a proficient non-native speaker or a native speaker of English to read the entire Prator Passage aloud for you. Did your friend use the intonation contours you expected in reading these particular sentences?

The Prator Passage was written many years ago and its content is related to non-native speakers studying at universities in the United States, so it may not be appropriate for learners in other countries or of other age groups, or for those who are studying English for non-academic purposes (such as business English or survival English for immigrant adults). You may want to revise this text somewhat or write a similar diagnostic passage that is more suitable for your learners.

Action

Write an original reading passage of your own which incorporates all the segmental phonemes and the major suprasegmental phonemes of English. The content and difficulty level should be appropriate for the learners you work with (or expect to work with in the future). Have a classmate or colleague read the text aloud for you to see if it produces the expected phonemes. With your friend, check your text against the vowel and consonant charts in Chapter 1, to make sure it contains at least one instance of every vowel and consonant sound in English.

8. Conclusion

In this chapter, we have considered the teaching of speaking to intermediate students. After the introduction we covered syllabus design issues, including the contrast between input-based and interaction-based lessons. Then in Section 3, we considered some principles to keep in mind when we are teaching speaking and pronunciation to intermediate learners. In Section 4, we looked at some sample materials and saw several task and exercise types for introducing and practicing speaking with intermediate learners. These included negotiation for meaning, developing transactional and interactional speech, and personalization. In Section 5, we focused specifically on pronunciation. Section 6 included a transcript of an extended lesson segment in which the teacher focused on developing an intermediate student's interactive speaking skills and his use of communication strategies. In the final section, we considered the assessment of speaking by intermediate students.

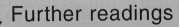

Further readings

Celce-Murcia, M. and E Olshtain. (2000). *Discourse and Context in Language Teaching: A Guide for Language Teachers.* Cambridge: Cambridge University Press.

> This book presumes some background knowledge on the part of the reader, but it has sections on phonology and speaking that will be helpful to language teachers.

Skillman P. and C. McMahill. (1996). *Springboard to Success: Communication Strategies for the Classroom and Beyond.* Upper Saddle River, NJ: Prentice Hall Regents.

> This textbook includes a whole unit for students on planning and performing a role-play.

Helpful Web sites

Online Pronunciation, Language Study Dictionary (www.fonetiks.org)

> This is a helpful Web site that was designed for English learners, so they could hear and learn about the sounds of different varieties of English. The Web site provides examples of British, Australian, Welsh, Irish, Canadian, Scottish, and American English pronunciation.

Pronunciation Web Resources (www.sunburstmedia.com/PronWeb.html)

> This Web site is especially helpful for teachers who want to learn more about teaching pronunciation.

References

The American Council on the Teaching of Foreign Languages (ACTFL)

Dell. 2000. *Dell Logic Puzzles.* Norwalk, CT: Dell Magazines, Crosstown Publications.

Fotos, S. 1995. Communicative tasks for grammar consciousness-raising. In M. Pennington (ed.), *New Ways in Teaching Grammar.* Alexandria, VA: TESOL, 135–154.

Kozyrev, J.R. 1998. *Talk It Up! Oral Communication for the Real World.* Boston, MA: Houghton Mifflin.

Krashen, S.D. 1985. *The Input Hypothesis: Issues and Implications.* London: Longman.

Long, M.H. 1983. Native Speaker/Non-native Speaker Conversation in the Second Language Classroom. In M.A. Clarke and J. Handscomb (eds.), *On TESOL '82: Pacific Perspectives on Language Learning and Teaching*. Washington D.C.: TESOL, 207–225.

Martinez, R. 1997. *Conversation Lessons: The Natural Language of Conversations (An Intermediate Course)*. Hove, UK: Language Teaching Publications.

Nunan, D. 1991. *Language Teaching Methodology: A Textbook for Teachers*. New York, NY: Prentice Hall.

Nunan, D. 2005. *Practical English Language Teaching Grammar*. New York, NY: McGraw-Hill ESL/ELT.

Omaggio, A.C. 1982. The Relationship Between Personalized Classroom Talk and Teacher Effectiveness Ratings: Some Research Results. *Foreign Language Annals*, 14(4): 255–269.

Pica, T., R. Young, and C. Doughty. 1987. The Impact of Interaction on Comprehension. *TESOL Quarterly*, 21(4): 737–758.

Prator, C.H. and B.W. Robinett. 1985. *Manual of American English Pronunciation*. New York, NY: Holt, Rinehart, and Winston.

Richards, J., J. Platt, and H. Weber. 1985. *Longman Dictionary of Applied Linguistics*. London: Longman.

Schmidt, R. and S.N. Frota. 1986. Developing Basic Conversational Ability in a Second Language: A Case Study of an Adult Learner of Portuguese. In R.R. Day (ed.), *Talking to Learn: Conversation in Second Language Acquisition*. Rowley, MA: Newbury House, 237–326.

Swain, M. 1995. Three Functions of Output in Second Language Learning. In G. Cook and B. Seidlhofer (eds.), *Principles and Practice in Applied Linguistics: Studies in Honor of H.G. Widdowson*. Oxford: Oxford University Press, 125–144.

Tanka, J., P. Most, and L. Baker. 2002. *Interactions 1: Listening/Speaking* (4th ed.). New York, NY: McGraw-Hill Contemporary.

Answer Key (p. 94)

Action

In each blank below, indicate whether the preceding utterance is a confirmation check, a comprehension check, or a clarification request.

John: Yes, you were born in Seoul, in Korea. And you said you are a Christian?
      confirmation check (Hint: John is making sure he understands what Kims was saying earlier.)

Kim: Yes. Baptist. Is many Baptist church.

John: Oh, you mean in Seoul? There are many Baptist churches in Seoul?
      confirmation check (Hint: John—as the speaker for a moment—is making sure he has understood Kim's meaning.)

Kim: Yeah. And all Korea.

John: All Korea? <u>clarification request</u> (Hint: John is asking for more
information from Kim about her immediately preceding statement.)

Kim: Yeah. Many part, many Baptist church. You know, Pusan? Inchon?
Taejon? Seoul? Many city, many church. You know what I mean?
<u>confirmation check</u> (Hint: This comment comes from Kim, as the
speaker, to see if John has understood what she meant.)

John: Oh, okay, okay. So there are many cities in Korea, like Pusan and
Taejon and so on, and those cities have many Baptist churches—right?
<u>confirmation check</u> (Hint: This remark is made by John, as the speaker,
to see if he has correctly understood what Kim said.)

Answer Key to Logic Puzzle (pp. 104–105)

	C	J	K	M	R	8	9	10	11	12	Hb	Sh	Ta	Su	Pa
1st	0	X	X	X	X	X	X	0	X	X	0	X	X	X	X
2nd	X	X	X	X	0	X	X	X	X	0	X	X	0	X	X
3rd	X	0	X	X	X	0	X	X	X	X	X	X	X	0	X
4th	X	X	0	X	X	X	X	X	0	X	X	X	X	X	0
5th	X	X	X	0	X	X	0	X	X	X	X	0	X	X	X
Hb	0	X	X	X	X	X	X	X	X	X					
Sh	X	X	X	0	X	X	0	X	X	X					
Ta	X	X	X	X	0	X	X	X	X	0					
Su	X	0	X	X	X	0	X	X	X	X					
Pa	X	X	0	X	X	X	X	X	0	X					
8	X	0	X	X	X										
9	X	X	X	0	X										
10	0	X	X	X	X										
11	X	X	0	X	X										
12	X	X	X	X	0										

Chapter **Four**

Speaking for advanced level learners

At the end of this chapter, you should be able to:

✔ **describe** several speaking issues that typically concern advanced learners.

✔ **explain** the following key principles for supporting the teaching of speaking to advanced learners: combining fluency and accuracy, encouraging reasonable risks, and noticing the gap.

✔ **create** materials and activities based on the following task and activity types: conversations, information gaps and jigsaw activities, picture-based activities, extemporaneous speaking, role-plays, and simulations.

✔ **examine** pieces of classroom interaction and identify the principles underpinning the instructional sequences.

✔ **discuss** primary trait scoring as a means of assessing speaking in role-plays.

1. Introduction

Working with advanced learners can be challenging, especially, perhaps, for novice teachers. At this level students have so many strengths and so many difficult questions! Nevertheless, there is much that English teachers can do to help advanced learners improve their speaking skills.

In this chapter, we will explore aspects of teaching speaking to advanced students, including professionals who must speak English well for their careers. The chapter follows a pattern similar to the previous two, by looking briefly at syllabus design issues (Section 2) and underlying principles (Section 3), before considering specific activities and exercise types in Section 4. Then we will concentrate on teaching pronunciation (Section 5), before we move on to samples of classroom interaction (Section 6). Finally, Section 7 presents assessment issues.

What can advanced learners do in speaking English? According to the ACTFL guidelines, advanced level language learners are able to:

- satisfy the requirements of everyday situations and routine school and work requirements.
- handle with confidence but not with facility complicated tasks and social situations, such as elaborating, complaining, and apologizing.
- narrate and describe with some details, linking sentences together smoothly.
- communicate facts and talk casually about topics of current public and personal interest, using general vocabulary.
- be understood without difficulty by native interlocutors.

It should be noted that in the ACTFL system, there are actually four major levels of assessment: novice, intermediate, advanced, and superior. These categories underscore the point that even advanced level speakers can still have room for improvement.

Reflection

Think about a non-native speaker you know whom you consider to be an advanced learner of English. What are the characteristics of that person's speech that make you think of him or her as "advanced"?

Talk to three advanced learners of English. According to these learners, what are their main goals for studying English? Focus specifically on spoken English. What are their current strengths? What areas do they most want to improve upon next? Now think about your own assessment of these people's speaking skills? What do you think are their current strengths in speaking English? What areas should they work to improve first? Fill out the chart below:

Which person	His/Her ideas	Your ideas
Learner #1		
Learner #2		
Learner #3		

Where your ideas differ from those of the individual learners, what accounts for the differences?

2. Syllabus design issues

As noted in earlier chapters, sometimes a syllabus is more or less set by the contents of the required textbook. At other times, a syllabus is designed by the program staff members, who then select or develop materials to achieve the goals of that syllabus. In some cases, the learners' own views are considered in developing or modifying a syllabus, often through **needs assessment**. This is a systematic process for determining the learners' needs and goals. It can include questionnaires with open-ended questions and/or items for rating or ranking. Sometimes the procedure involves interviewing students or their employers (or future employers). No matter how a needs assessment is done, the process can produce valuable information for shaping your syllabus.

It could be argued that needs assessments are even more important at the advanced levels than they are for beginning or intermediate students. It is especially important that very proficient students (who are already capable of getting their needs met and communicating their ideas effectively) should be involved in determining what kinds of instruction is most appropriate for them, because advanced level learners have had considerable experience of learning and using the language. When you are working with advanced learners, it is important to take their goals and concerns into consideration. They often have specific goals for improving their English, and you can sustain that motivation by helping them meet those goals.

Here is a simple needs assessment plan that can help you and your learners decide what to focus on in planning a syllabus (Peter Shaw, personal communication; Beck, 1983). First list the speaking skills you think the learners will need to develop, or brainstorm such a list with your students. If you create the list yourself, be sure to leave some blank rows where the students can add other issues that arise during your class discussion.

Figure 1 is based on students learning English for academic purposes. The instructions to the students are to indicate the importance, difficulty, and frequency of each skill by writing "high," "medium," or "low" in the cells to the right. As an alternative, you could use a point scale of one (low importance, difficulty, or frequency) to five (high importance, difficulty, or frequency) if you wished to average the students' ratings. Figure 1 below gives an example of an individual learner's needs assessment.

Speaking Skill or Task	Importance	Difficulty	Frequency
1. Asking questions in class	high	medium	high
2. Doing group projects in English	high	medium	high
3. Giving panel presentations	high	high	low
4. Talking on the telephone	high	medium	high
5. Conversing with classmates	medium	low	high
6. Giving extemporaneous speeches	high	high	low
7. Other: Meeting a professor in office hours	high	medium	low
8. Other:			
9. Other:			

Figure 1 Sample needs assessment form for learners in an advanced speaking course

When individual students have completed the needs assessment chart, you can have them work in small groups to compare their analyses of the speaking skills. Then a delegate of each group can present the members' opinions to the entire class.

As an alternative, if you have groups of three people, one person can move one group to the right, and another can move one group to the left, while the third person stays in place. In this way, the groups are totally reformed with new participants, who then share the needs assessment ideas from their former group with their new partners.

Finally, you can collect each person's needs assessment chart and compile the results from the whole class. In this way, you can solicit your students' input about prioritizing the speaking skills they wish to develop. Figure 2 below provides an example of such a compilation from a class of thirty students.

Speaking Skill or Task	Importance	Difficulty	Frequency
1. Asking questions in class	high (28) medium (2) low (0)	high (10) medium (18) low (2)	high (13) medium (4) low (3)
2. Doing group projects in English	high (20) medium (10) low (0)	high (10) medium (13) low (7)	high (17) medium (10) low (3)
3. Giving panel presentations	high (6) medium (22) low (2)	high (14) medium (16) low (0)	high (6) medium (6) low (18)
4. Talking on the telephone	high (24) medium (6) low (0)	high (20) medium (6) low (4)	high (28) medium (2) low (0)
5. Conversing with classmates	high (10) medium (15) low (5)	high (2) medium (4) low (24)	high (27) medium (3) low (0)
6. Giving extemporaneous speeches	high (24) medium (6) low (0)	high (28) medium (2) low (0)	high (20) medium (10) low (0)
7. Other: Meeting a professor in office hours	high (1)	medium (1)	low (1)
8. Other: Having a job interview in English	high (3)	high (3)	low (3)
9. Other:			

Figure 2 Compilation of the needs assessment forms for 30 students in an advanced speaking course

3. Principles for teaching speaking to advanced learners

In Chapters 2 and 3 we considered important principles for teaching speaking to beginning students, false beginners, and intermediate students. Those ideas are also important with more proficient learners. Now, in this section, we will examine three additional key principles for teaching speaking to advanced learners:

- Help learners to combine fluency and accuracy.
- Encourage learners to take reasonable risks in speaking English.
- Provide opportunities for learners to notice the gap.

These principles are helpful for teaching learners at all levels, but in my experience advanced students can make great gains in these areas.

1. Help learners to combine fluency and accuracy.

In previous chapters we have talked about activities for helping learners develop **fluency** and **accuracy**, but not about how to work on these two goals at the same time. At the advanced levels it is important that the learners are able to speak English spontaneously at a normal conversational rate, but also that they maintain their accuracy as they do so.

What do we mean by *fluency* and *accuracy*? These terms were introduced in Chapter 1, but let's revisit and refine our definitions. In this book, I have adopted the position taken by Hammerly:

> Although the word 'fluency' has long been used in everyday speech to mean speaking rapidly *and well,* in our field it has largely come to mean speaking rapidly and smoothly but not necessarily grammatically. (1991, p. 12)

In contrast, accuracy involves control over "the linguistic code" (ibid.)– using the rules of the language. Being a truly proficient speaker of a language involves speaking creatively and spontaneously, while being both fluent and accurate. In Section 4 of this chapter, we will consider some activities designed to promote fluency and accuracy.

2. Encourage learners to take reasonable risks in English.

Sometimes advanced learners get comfortable with their level of proficiency and seem to stop trying to improve their English. After all, they have a functional range of vocabulary and can generally make themselves understood and get their needs met. They have mastered many English grammar patterns. They have probably also developed a number of communication strategies, which help them to carry on conversations in spite of inevitable gaps in their vocabulary and knowledge of grammar rules.

There are several ways to stretch learners' proficiency at these higher levels by encouraging them to try new things and take reasonable risks in speaking English. For example, in my work with university students in the U.S., needs analyses have often shown that such learners are hesitant to ask their professors questions during lectures and seminar discussions. Perhaps these students are self-conscious about speaking in front of their native speaker classmates and other proficient non-native speakers. Maybe they come from academic cultures where it is not considered polite to question professors. Getting these learners to ask questions in class and providing them with strategies for doing so involves encouraging them to take reasonable risks.

Of course, there are other kinds of reasonable risks that advanced learners can be encouraged to take. Talking with a stranger in English, attending a party where English is spoken, participating in a job interview, or giving a talk to a civic organization in English can all be growth experiences. Your role as a teacher may simply be to help the students prepare and rehearse in order to gain fluency and confidence.

Reflection

Think of three things you could do as an ESL/EFL teacher to help university students who are not native speakers of English to ask questions during English-medium classes with instructors other than you. Write down your ideas and share them with a colleague or classmate.

3. Provide opportunities for learners to notice the gap.

What does it mean to say that learners should be given opportunities to **"notice the gap"** (Schmidt and Frota, 1986, pp. 310–315)? This phrase describes an experience that people have when they are interacting in a second or foreign language. It refers to the learner realizing that the way he is saying something in the target language differs from the way native or proficient speakers say it. This awareness can be about individual words, grammar rules, idioms, appropriate phrases, pronunciation–any component of the language she is learning. Some researchers (e.g., Schmidt and Frota, 1986) believe that this awareness must occur before a learner can make the necessary adjustments in her developing competence.

The idea of noticing the gap is not the same as monitoring one's own output (Krashen, 1985). The concept of **monitoring** refers to learners checking what they say or write, based on rules they've already learned. Monitoring may lead learners to notice the gap, but this experience can happen in the *absence* of known rules. Noticing the gap can involve the learner's realization that he *doesn't* know the word or the structure he is trying to say.

In fact, the phrase "notice the gap" has also been used with the idea of learners realizing that there is a difference between what they want to say and what they can say. This process involves the development of linguistic self-awareness on the learner's part. There are many things that we as teachers can do to help learners become more self-aware. Some of these ideas will be discussed in Section 4, when we consider some tasks and materials for speaking activities.

Reflection

Think of a time when you were speaking a language other than your own and you noticed you couldn't say what you wanted to, or that the way you were saying it was different from what more proficient or native speakers were saying. What did you notice? What made you notice the gap?

Sometimes such awareness occurs when we are trying to be both accurate and fluent, or when we are taking risks in the target language. Was that the case when you noticed a gap in your speaking? Describe your experience to a classmate or colleague.

If possible, talk to two advanced learners of English. Ask them each to tell you about some times when they (1) knowingly tried to combine fluency and accuracy (when they were speaking spontaneously), (2) took a reasonable risk in speaking English, and (3) noticed a gap in their English speaking. What, if any, are the common themes in their experiences?

4. Tasks and materials

The purpose of this section is to describe and illustrate some task and activity types that can be used with advanced learners. These activities also illustrate the key principles described above. The following task and exercise types are discussed in this section:

1. Conversations and other interactions
2. Information gap and jigsaw activities
3. Picture-based activities
4. Extemporaneous speaking
5. Role-plays and simulations

1. Conversations and other interactions

Conversations are one of the most basic forms of human interaction. On ordinary days, most people participate in many different conversations. The processes involved are so mundane and so commonplace that we normally don't notice them until something goes wrong, as it often does if we are speaking a language other than our native language. Even advanced level learners can experience difficulties in carrying on a conversation. In addition talking with others is an important way to continue the language acquisition process. For these reasons, it is important that teachers help advanced learners continue to develop their conversational skills.

Sometimes so-called 'conversation classes' involve the teacher simply talking with the learners, without any plan for teaching students about *how* to converse in English. However, we can actually focus on the rules of conversation as well. Example 1 is some advice from a popular textbook for advanced learners:

Example 1

Starting a Conversation (Audio)

There are several ways to start a conversation with someone you know. One way is to ask a question about what the person has been doing lately. Here are some examples:

- What have you been doing lately?
- What have you guys been up to lately?
- So what's new?
- How was your weekend?

Friends give each other honest answers; the answer usually leads to more conversation. Here is an example:

A: What have you been doing lately?

B: I was at the library all weekend. I have a big exam next week.

   OR:

   Well, I saw a great movie last night.

   Um, I went to the beach on Sunday.

Either Speaker A or Speaker B can continue the conversation by asking another question. Here are some examples:

A: What have you been doing lately?

B: Well, I saw a great movie last night.

A: Oh . . . what did you see?

A: How was your weekend?

B: Great. How was yours?

Quest: Listening and Speaking in the Academic World, Book One
(Hartmann and Blass, 2000, p. 115)

As an in-class activity, you can write the bulleted questions in Example 1 on slips of paper and distribute them at random to your students. Using the cocktail party technique described in Chapter 2 (p. 40), have students practice asking and replying to these conversation starters. Redistribute the slips of paper several times, so that each student gets to practice different opening lines.

Action

With a classmate or colleague, brainstorm three to five more conversation starters that would be appropriate for advanced learners to use to begin a conversation.

Advanced learners are often adept at conversing about familiar topics in English. Talking about unfamiliar or abstract topics or conversing with strangers can be more risky. Also, advanced learners will need to participate in important situated interactions, such as job interviews, staff meetings, and academic seminars. These situations often involve risks for language learners because the outcome of these communications may be quite important.

Let us return to the example of advanced students who must be able to ask questions and make comments during university seminars and lectures. What can be done to encourage these students to ask questions in their classes and seminars? Here are some procedures I have found useful in the past:

1. Help the students master the grammar patterns they need in order to ask appropriate and accurate questions in class. ("Could you please repeat/define/explain...?")

2. Provide the students with useful politeness formulae for asking questions. This activity can include worksheets with examples of how to politely get the speaker's attention. ("Excuse me, Professor Smith, could you please...?")

3. Set up a practice activity in which you are the lecturer or seminar leader. Each student must ask a question about what you have said. (Keep track of who has asked a question and who has not. Sometimes to playfully utilize the available peer pressure, I have told students they cannot have a recess until everyone in the class has asked at least one question.)

4. Bring in a guest speaker who is a (supportive) stranger to talk to your students. Again, the students must each ask an appropriate question of the speaker while he or she is lecturing. You can have them brainstorm a possible list of questions first in groups or pairs.

These steps illustrate activities for getting advanced learners to take a reasonable risk and ask questions in their classes. For those learners who are not university students, reasonable risks to take will be determined by their own contexts. For instance, in an EFL situation, secondary school students might decide to watch an entire movie in English without subtitles or voice over dialogue in their native language. (The risk is that they may be confused or bored in some parts of the film.)

2. Information gap and jigsaw activities: The fluency relay

Activities involving **information gaps** can be used at all levels of instruction to create communicative needs and motivate interaction. Here is an activity for advanced level learners that uses **manipulables** and encourages creativity and clarity in conveying specific information. In this activity, learners must take some risks and try to be both fluent and accurate. The activity also provides many opportunities for learners to use comprehension checks, clarification requests, and confirmation checks (see Chapter 3).

This activity is the "fluency relay." It is like a relay race in which runners pass a baton to other teammates. But in this activity, what is passed along is information. It is an ideal procedure for working on both fluency and accuracy, since the competitive nature of the relay lends a sense of urgency to the communication, but participants must also be precise in order to be successful.

The fluency relay can be done with any kind of manipulables, but I like to use the children's plastic toys called Legos™ because when you snap them together they will stay in place. You will build a structure out of Legos and, using an information gap task, teams of students will try to duplicate it. This relay is more complex—linguistically and interactionally—than the information gap and jigsaw activities we have seen in the earlier chapters of this book.

Begin by dividing your students into teams of three people each. The teams are each given exactly the same number of Lego pieces that you have. Each team's pieces must also be identical to yours in shape, size, and color. (You can also use Cuisenaire Rods, coins, bits of colored paper, or sticks and seedpods, as long as each team has an identical set of manipulables.)

In the fluency relay, each team has a Watcher, a Runner, and a Builder. Divide the room (or the teaching space) into zones. Put the Builders at the back of the room. The Watchers are stationed at the front of the room, near the teacher's desk or table. The Runners are stationed between the Builders and the Watchers. The space for the Runners' zone should be about twice the width of the space for the Watchers:

Teacher's Desk Area	Watchers' Zone	Runners' Zone	Builders' Table

During the relay every member of each team has a particular job to do. While you are building the Lego structure behind a podium or a large book standing on end (so that what you are building is hidden from the view of the Runners and the Builders), the Watchers closely observe the process and the emerging structure. The Runners are not allowed to come into the Watchers' zone and cannot see what you are doing. Each Watcher then tells the Runner from his own team about the structure you are building. Next the Runner tells the Builder for his team what the Watcher said, so the Builder can reconstruct the figure. (It is important that the Runners cannot see what the Builders are doing.) Typically the Builder has questions (e.g., about the orientation of the various Lego pieces), so the Runner goes back to the Watcher's zone and conveys those questions to the Watcher on his team. The Runner then brings back the Watcher's answer to the Builder. In this way, the Runners must communicate a great deal of information about the original structure and the duplicate structure without ever having seen either of them!

The object of the fluency relay is for the Builders to reproduce exactly the structure that the teacher has constructed. The challenge arises in that (1) the Builders have never seen the model structure; (2) the Builders must rely on the Runners' guidance; (3) the Runners have never seen the model structure; and (4) the Runners must rely on the Watchers' guidance. Of course, in addition to the linguistic challenge here, this task demands a great deal of teamwork and cooperation. (In fact, this "game" is used to train native speakers who must work together on corporate or human resources teams, to demonstrate the value of teamwork and clear communication.)

You can turn this game into systematic communication strategies practice by repeating three or more rounds of the fluency relay. In Round A, the builders are given five or six Lego pieces. The task and the roles are new to all the participants. There is no formal viewing of or labeling of the Lego pieces prior to beginning the task.

In Round B, the participants are allowed to view the pieces and label them before the relay begins. The students typically come up with names like "the little red chimney" or "the yellow car battery" or "the thin flat blue piece" and so on. This process provides shared meaning and builds teamwork.

In Round C, the teacher should provide time for the teams to meet first, to discuss what communication strategies worked well and where they had trouble expressing and understanding ideas. Together the students come up with strategies for communicating about the Lego pieces and the particular structures the teacher might build with them. For example, instead of just saying that a piece extends out, a Watcher might say, "It is sticking out like a diving board." This is also a good activity for getting students to work with analogies, similes, and metaphors in the target language.

Action

Try this fluency relay with three of your classmates or colleagues before using it with language students. When you try it, think about these questions:
- What sorts of negotiation for meaning took place between (a) the Watchers and the Runners, and (b) the Runners and the Builders?
- Which communication strategies were successful and which were less successful?

Ask the team members if they experienced any frustration, confusion, triumph, anxiety, satisfaction, anger, annoyance, boredom, fatigue, or other emotional responses during this activity.

Here is a plan for rotating the roles so that three people (1, 2, and 3) each have a chance to be a Runner (R), a Builder (B), and a Watcher (W) over three rounds (A, B, and C) of the activity:

Person → Round ↓	1	2	3
A	R	B	W
B	W	R	B
C	B	W	R

If you have extra students, I suggest you have two Watchers and/or two Runners, but just one Builder, since the Builders may have to wait sometimes while the Runners and the Watchers negotiate.

You can make the activity more challenging by adding new Lego pieces after the first round. It is also interesting to switch or remove pieces from the structure once you've put them in place. Doing so creates more challenges for the teams.

3. Picture-based activities for teaching speaking

Here is a picture-based activity that can be used with advanced learners, either singly or in pairs. It works well whether the students are from different countries or the same place. The activity builds on travel and tourism, as well as the students' pride in and knowledge of their own countries or home regions. Start with pictures of famous scenes and beautiful places from the learners' country or home region.

Context: The students work individually or in small groups to produce a persuasive speech. The point is to try to convince a large travel agency to bring a group of tourists to a certain place. This activity works best if that place is represented by a large and attractive picture.

Pictures: Use calendar photos or other large format pictures. (If your students are making PowerPoint presentations, the photos can be displayed on a large-format screen.) The pictures represent locations in the students' home country or region. As an alternative, if the learners have been studying geography, political science, or world history, the pictures can depict the areas they have been investigating.

Speaking task: Working alone, in pairs, or in groups of three, students must produce the notes for a speech to be presented to the travel agency staff, who will decide where to take the tourists. The individual student or a member of the group then presents the ideas orally to the class. The class members may vote on the best presentation, as if they were the travel agency representatives.

Variations in the audience: The travel agency may represent a particular kind of tourist group. For example, the tourists may be members of a photographers' club, college professors, hiking enthusiasts, elderly people, etc. In this instance, the learners must tailor their persuasive speaking to fit the interests of the particular group of tourists.

It may be helpful for you as the teacher to establish categories of information the students should include in their speech—for example, climate, scenic beauty, tourist attractions, ease of transportation, etc. Or, you could get the class to brainstorm the information categories that would be important to use in such a presentation. You can also elicit from the students some appropriate vocabulary to be used in discussing each of these topics, or pre-teach terms as necessary.

In doing this project, the students will gain a great deal of speaking practice, but you can add a writing component to this activity as well. Working alone, in pairs, or in groups of three, students must produce a letter or a brochure to be sent to the travel agency staff, who will decide where to take the tourists. If this project will be used as a lengthy assignment about the learners' home city, region or territory, the students may produce a brochure with photographs they have taken or drawings they have made. They can also cut out pictures from magazines. As an alternative, the students could prepare a PowerPoint presentation with photos downloaded from the Internet.

4. Extemporaneous speaking

Many advanced level learners need to be able to make coherent speeches in English to an audience, often an audience of strangers. Such situations include international students participating in seminars, scholarship recipients speaking to civic groups, visiting scholars attending scientific conferences, employees escorting visitors at a factory, and business people involved in marketing a product or negotiating a contract.

Speaking with preparation is called **extemporaneous speaking**. It contrasts with **impromptu speaking**, which is spontaneous and involves little or no preparation. Effective extemporaneous speakers know how to prepare, so that what is actually a planned speech seems to be a natural and relaxed presentation.

Speaking in front of an audience can be an uncomfortable experience, even when we are using our native language. For learners speaking in a second or foreign language, it can be doubly nerve-wracking. Nevertheless, being able to speak extemporaneously is an essential skill and one that can definitely be learned. Here is some advice for advanced level learners about preparing and giving a speech.

Example 2

 speaking **Strategy**

Giving a Speech to the Class

You will occasionally need to give a speech in front of the class. These suggestions will help you give an effective presentation.

- Prepare, prepare, prepare. Organize your ideas and write your speech as you would organize an essay.
- Don't memorize what you are going to say. If necessary, though, you might memorize short pieces. For example, you might memorize a quotation or a few lines of a poem.
- Put *just notes* on 3 × 5 index cards. These notes might be the first few words of each section of your speech, or they might be phrases that you are afraid you will forget.
- Practice your speech several times at home. Present your speech to a friend or family member or even to your bathroom mirror.
- During your speech, glance at your index cards whenever you need help remembering something.
- As you're speaking, have eye contact with the people in your audience, the people to whom you're speaking. If it makes you nervous to have eye contact, look at people's foreheads instead of their eyes.
- Don't forget to breathe.

Quest: Listening and Speaking in the Academic World, Book One
(Hartmann and Blass, 2000, pp. 102-103)

When learners must give a speech in another language, it's important that teachers give them a wide range of choices regarding what they talk about. Researching an unfamiliar topic adds to the work load and possibly to the anxiety of public speaking. Your students will feel more confident if they can discuss a topic they know well. Here are some tips for advanced level learners about choosing a topic and determining the purpose for extemporaneous speaking:

Example 3

A. Selecting and Limiting Your Topic

In a professional situation the topic of your presentation is usually determined by the needs of your listeners. You may be asked to provide certain information because of your specialized knowledge or your experience in a particular area. For example, you might have to demonstrate how something works, describe a technical process, compare two pieces of equipment made by different companies, or give on-the-job instructions.

A classroom situation differs from a professional situation in that you often have more freedom to choose your own topic for a class presentation. Of course, you should choose a topic that you already know something about, one that interests you, and one that is of potential interest to your listeners. You can choose a subject related to your work, your studies, your research projects, or your personal interests. Current events or social issues can also make good subjects for class presentations. Once you have chosen a general subject area, then you have to limit your topic so you can cover it adequately within the time available for your presentation. It is usually more effective to give a detailed explanation of a specific, limited topic than to try to cover too much material in a short time. When selecting your own topic for a class presentation, you should consider the following points:

1. Do you know enough about this topic?
2. If some research is needed, do you have the time and resources to find the information?
3. Have you limited the topic enough so that you can cover it adequately in the time available?
4. Is this topic of potential interest to your listeners?
5. Is the topic too difficult or too technical for this audience?
6. Is the topic too easy or too well-known to this audience?

B. Determining Your General Purpose

In giving a presentation, a speaker usually has one of three general purposes: to inform, to persuade, or to entertain the listeners. Most of the oral presentations that you need to give at work are reports to inform your listeners—to give them information that they want or need to know. Therefore, the focus in this course is on informative presentations. Your goal in giving any type of informative presentation is to communicate useful information in a clear way.

Professional Interactions: Oral Communicational Skills in Science, Technology, and Medicine (Matthews and Marino, 1990, pp. 56–57)

One helpful practice activity is to have students explain a process that they are completely familiar with and the audience is not. Explaining a process is an ideal topic for an extemporaneous speech, because the process has a beginning, two or more sequential steps, and a conclusion, which is often an observable outcome of some sort. The chronological order of the process provides a natural organization for the speech. Over the years my advanced speaking students have delivered very interesting presentations on such diverse topics as how silk is produced, how different golf clubs propel a golf ball, and how to make sushi. Example 4 is a list of simple discourse structures you can provide to help your students get started on their speeches.

> ### Example 4
>
> 1. Good morning ladies and gentlemen. In this presentation I will explain how to…
> 2. This is an important topic because…
> 3. To begin, we…
> 4. Second, ….
> 5. Third, ….
> 6. Finally, ….
> 7. So, as you can see…
> 8. In closing, then, …

Having the students choose topics that they are familiar with but the audience is not is important for three reasons. First, the "expert status" of the speakers gives them a reason to communicate: they have knowledge which the audience lacks. Second, their familiarity with the topic may help bolster their confidence while speaking in a foreign language. Third, if they are describing processes they know intimately, they do not have to focus so much on what they are saying and can concentrate instead on how to say it.

Giving an extemporaneous speech in English is an example of taking a reasonable risk. The learners can prepare before the speech and in doing so they may notice some gaps in what they are trying to say. And giving the speech in class to their teacher and their peers before they present it to strangers can help increase their fluency, accuracy, and confidence. Of course, if you videotape the students' presentations, they can review their presentations later, either with or without your input.

Action

Choose a process with which you are very familiar, to use as the basis of an extemporaneous speech. The topic can be a hobby, a recipe you know well, a process in a sport (e.g., how to line up a pool cue), a mundane household chore (e.g. how to start a washing machine), a skill related to gardening or arts and crafts—any process you could explain to someone who doesn't know about it. Use the eight phrases from Example 4 to frame a speech about the process you've chosen.

If you speak a second language, try giving the same speech in that language. It would be ideal if you could give your extemporaneous speech to proficient or native speakers of that language to get their feedback.

5. Role-plays and simulations

At the advanced level, in-class role-plays and simulations are extremely important for several reasons. First, advanced learners can tell you the situations, topics, and speech acts that are challenging for them, so you can design role-plays and simulations that represent those contexts. Second, doing role-plays and simulations during class meetings gives students opportunities to try out their English speaking skills in a safe environment where they can receive immediate feedback from supportive individuals who understand their concerns (i.e., the teacher and their classmates). Third, in a role-play or simulation, people have the chance to try it again—to "rewind the tape," so to speak—and redo the interaction with improvements, an opportunity we seldom have in real life. Fourth, during a role-play or simulation—particularly if it is audio or video-recorded—the learners can analyze their own production (with or without input from the teacher) and notice the gaps in their English. (See Ladousse, 1987.)

Role-plays and simulations are particularly useful for practicing speech acts. Learners at advanced levels of English proficiency will be involved in a wide range of interactions, and will need to use many different speech acts appropriately. One challenging set of speech acts consists of expressing agreement or disagreement. Here are some examples from a widely used textbook for advanced learners.

Example 5

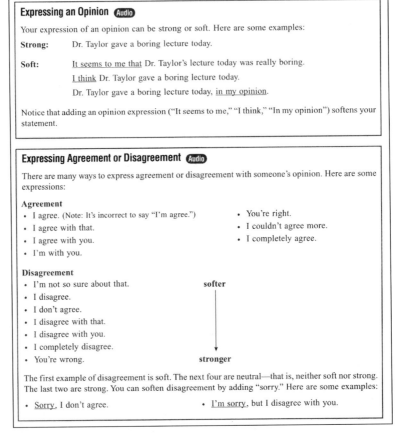

Expressing an Opinion (Audio)

Your expression of an opinion can be strong or soft. Here are some examples:

Strong: Dr. Taylor gave a boring lecture today.

Soft: It seems to me that Dr. Taylor's lecture today was really boring.

  I think Dr. Taylor gave a boring lecture today.

  Dr. Taylor gave a boring lecture today, in my opinion.

Notice that adding an opinion expression ("It seems to me," "I think," "In my opinion") softens your statement.

Expressing Agreement or Disagreement (Audio)

There are many ways to express agreement or disagreement with someone's opinion. Here are some expressions:

Agreement
- I agree. (Note: It's incorrect to say "I'm agree.")
- I agree with that.
- I agree with you.
- I'm with you.
- You're right.
- I couldn't agree more.
- I completely agree.

Disagreement
- I'm not so sure about that.
- I disagree.
- I don't agree.
- I disagree with that.
- I disagree with you.
- I completely disagree.
- You're wrong.

softer

↓

stronger

The first example of disagreement is soft. The next four are neutral—that is, neither soft nor strong. The last two are strong. You can soften disagreement by adding "sorry." Here are some examples:

- Sorry, I don't agree.
- I'm sorry, but I disagree with you.

Quest: Listening and Speaking in the Academic World, Book One
(Hartmann and Blass, 2000, p. 45)

Expressing disagreement appropriately can be especially difficult. If a learner disagrees too tentatively, he may not make his point. On the other hand, if the learner disagrees too strongly, he may offend his listener. Here is some advice from a book for advanced learners on how to disagree politely in talking with English speakers.

Example 6

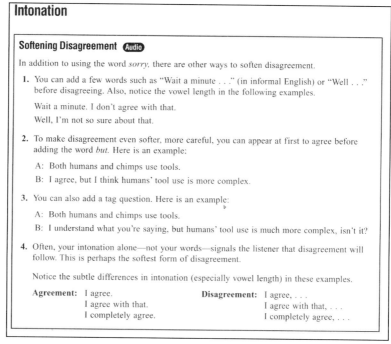

Intonation

Softening Disagreement (Audio)

In addition to using the word *sorry*, there are other ways to soften disagreement.

1. You can add a few words such as "Wait a minute . . ." (in informal English) or "Well . . ." before disagreeing. Also, notice the vowel length in the following examples.

   Wait a minute. I don't agree with that.
   Well, I'm not so sure about that.

2. To make disagreement even softer, more careful, you can appear at first to agree before adding the word *but*. Here is an example:

   A: Both humans and chimps use tools.
   B: I agree, but I think humans' tool use is more complex.

3. You can also add a tag question. Here is an example:

   A: Both humans and chimps use tools.
   B: I understand what you're saying, but humans' tool use is much more complex, isn't it?

4. Often, your intonation alone—not your words—signals the listener that disagreement will follow. This is perhaps the softest form of disagreement.

   Notice the subtle differences in intonation (especially vowel length) in these examples.

   Agreement: I agree.   **Disagreement:** I agree, . . .
   I agree with that.   I agree with that, . . .
   I completely agree.   I completely agree, . . .

Quest: Listening and Speaking in the Academic World, Book One (Hartmann and Blass, 2000, p. 46)

These examples of softening disagreement can be very useful in natural conversations, as well as in role-plays. They can also be helpful in groupwork or pairwork with logic puzzles when the participants disagree with one another.

A useful lesson on disagreeing politely for intermediate and advanced learners can be found in Dörnyei and Thurrell (1992). The steps for the lesson are clearly spelled out, beginning with, "Ask students to imagine they are talking to someone like an elderly neighbor or relative, their headteacher or boss, their driving instructor, or a stranger who is older than them, and they disagree strongly with what that person is saying" (p. 90). In this way, the learners are reminded of the importance of **register**. The lesson materials provide a helpful list of expressions for disagreeing politely, including the following:

Example 7

I agree with you, but...
Agreed/Granted, but...
That's a good idea, but...
That's one way of looking at it, but...
Yes, but don't you think...?
I think perhaps it's more a case of...
But surely...
Forgive me if I'm wrong, but...
I don't think it's quite that simple; you see...
Personally, I wouldn't go so far as (to say) that...

Adapted from Dörnyei and Thurrell, 1992, p. 91

After your students have been introduced to appropriate ways of agreeing and disagreeing in English, you can provide practice opportunities by writing role-play scenarios. For example, two students can have a conversation about what to do on a class outing and how to organize the event. One person wants the class to have pizza and go to a movie one evening and the other wants the class to go for a walk and have a picnic on a weekend day. Encourage the students to talk for at least five minutes without compromising, so that they can practice disagreeing appropriately.

Reflection

What sort of language (vocabulary, grammatical structures, speech acts) would you expect the learners to need in order to do this role-play successfully? What language would you pre-teach in setting up the role-play task?

Ask two students to do this role-play, and record them doing it, if possible. Did the learners use some of the language you predicted? In light of your experience, how would you set up the role-play next time?

A **simulation** is more elaborate than a role-play. According to Jones (1982, pp. 4–7), a simulation contains three essential elements: (1) reality of function, (2) a simulated environment, and (3) explicit structure.

First, reality of function means that participants "must mentally accept the function the simulation requires of them" (p. 4). Instead of thinking of themselves as students, "they must step inside the function mentally and behaviourally, and do the best they can to carry out their duties and responsibilities" (ibid.) of their role in the simulation. So, for instance, if the simulation calls for the learner to be a professor accusing a student of plagiarism, the learner should take on the professor's responsibilities in that situation.

Second, there must be a simulated environment that is as realistic as possible, but is still separate from the real world. It is this characteristic that makes simulations safe for the participants and creates an ideal context for taking reasonable risks. In this regard, simulations require more "props" than role-plays do (e.g., documents, information, furnishings, authentic texts, etc.).

Third, simulations must be explicitly structured around some realistic problem. The teacher provides the conditions and the context for the learners (unlike in a role-play, where the participants themselves sometimes invent some of the conditions). Thus a simulation can be defined as "reality of function in a simulated and structured environment" (p. 5).

Let's consider an example related to extemporaneous speaking. Many advanced learners will need to be able to speak to an audience, and the members of that audience may be unknown (and even unpredictable) to a speaker. As the teacher, you can certainly have students practice giving extemporaneous speeches in class. But you could also set up a simulated conference as follows:

1. Have each learner prepare a five to eight minute speech. The topic can be related to a particular theme, if that is appropriate for your learners.
2. The speakers should choose a descriptive title and write a fifty-word summary of their presentation.
3. You produce and print a "program" that provides each speaker's name, the title of the presentation, and the summary. The program also shows who speaks and in which order.
4. You assign specific roles to those class members who are not speaking. These roles could include the timekeeper, the heckler, the devoted follower, the skeptic, and so on.
5. The speaker gives his or her presentation complete with overhead projector transparencies, handouts, and/or PowerPoint slides.
6. After each student gives his or her speech, the audience members should ask questions or make comments in the persona of the assigned role. The question-and-answer period should last five to eight minutes.
7. It can be useful to have some class members take the role of observers. Instead of participating in the question-and-answer period after the speech, the observers focus specifically on (a) the quality of the presentation, and (b) how well the speaker deals with the questions and comments.

Setting up a mock-conference in this way provides a realistic opportunity for students to gain valuable experience before they must participate in a real conference. Thus, simulations can be used to encourage learners to take reasonable risks. (See also Crookall and Arai, 1995.)

5. Teaching pronunciation

At the advanced level, learners of English typically have a good range of vocabulary words, general command over grammar rules, and well developed communication strategies. Often, however, they will want to improve their pronunciation. This is not an easy undertaking, but it is not impossible either.

We saw in the earlier chapters that when native speakers use English quickly and/or casually, some sounds are reduced or blended. When this happens it can be difficult for English learners to understand what is being said, so practice with understanding reduced forms is important at all levels. For advanced learners, however, it will also be important to learn how to produce reduced forms in casual speech. Of course, it is important to enunciate clearly enough to be understood. But, ironically, if learners' speech is too precise, they may be viewed as bookish, "stuffy," or aloof. Here are some sample exercises on reduced forms:

Example 8

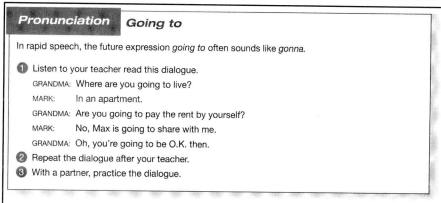

Pronunciation *Have to* and *has to*

In rapid speech, *have to* sounds like *hafta* and *has to* sounds like *hasta*.

1. Listen to your teacher read this dialogue.

   TV INTERVIEWER: What does the government have to do?

   UNION LEADER: The government has to protect workers.

   TV INTERVIEWER: What do the workers have to do?

   UNION LEADER: Workers have to speak with one voice.

   TV INTERVIEWER: And you provide that voice?

   UNION LEADER: We help the workers explain their needs. They don't have to worry.

2. Repeat the dialogue after your teacher.

3. With a partner, practice the dialogue.

Pronunciation *Going to*

In rapid speech, the future expression *going to* often sounds like *gonna*.

1. Listen to your teacher read this dialogue.

   GRANDMA: Where are you going to live?

   MARK: In an apartment.

   GRANDMA: Are you going to pay the rent by yourself?

   MARK: No, Max is going to share with me.

   GRANDMA: Oh, you're going to be O.K. then.

2. Repeat the dialogue after your teacher.

3. With a partner, practice the dialogue.

React, Interact: Situations for Communication (Byrd and Clemente, 2001, pp. 61 & 133)

    This kind of dialogue has many applications. You can say the long form and have students say the short form. Or students can practice giving the long and short forms to one another. They can also listen for instances of the more casual reduced forms outside of class during conversations or in films, television programs, or radio broadcasts.

    One difficult pronunciation issue for both understanding and producing spoken American English is the difference between *can* and *can't*. Here is some advice about comprehending these words from a textbook for advanced learners:

Example 9

Can and Can't [Audio]

In some cases, the words *can* and *can't* might sound the same to you because you don't always hear the *-t* in *can't*. This is especially true when a word beginning with *-t* or *-d* follows these words. Three suggestions follow:

1. Use the context to help you understand. Here is an example:

    "I'm sorry, but I can't talk right now."

2. You can ask for clarification. Here is an example:

    Did you say *can* or *can't?*

3. Listen for stress and the vowel sound: Is it the full /æ/ sound in *can't* or the reduced /ə/ sound in *can?* Don't worry about the *-t* at the end.

Quest: Listening and Speaking in the Academic World, Book One (Hartmann and Blass, 2000, p. 214)

It is important to distinguish between *can* and *can't* in both speaking and listening because confusing the two can lead to communication breakdowns. In rapid or casual spoken American English, *can* is shorter in duration than *can't.* Sometimes it sounds more like a contracted syllable than a separate word:

Written Form	**Casual Spoken Form**
I can see it.	I c'n see it.
He can manage.	He c'n manage.
They can buy it.	They c'n buy it.
You can do it.	You c'n do it.

The exercise in Example 9 emphasizes listening, but the same informa-tion can be used for speaking practice in pairwork or a role-play. Give a pair of students two conflicting schedules for the week and have them try to arrange a time for an hour-long meeting without showing each other their cal-endars. As the learners use *can* and *can't* in their utterances, they practice with these forms in a situation where pronunciation makes a meaning difference. Here are some example utterances that students might use:

Student A: Can you meet at ten on Monday morning?
Student B: No, I can't. I have a class. Can you meet at two that after-noon?

Student A: No, I can't. I have an appointment with my professor. Can you meet at four?

Student B: No, I can't. I have a chemistry lab then.

You should arrange for the partners to have two calendars with several conflicts already scheduled. (That is, where Student A has an open hour, Student B has an important class, and vice versa.) But also be sure to leave some open hours in the students' schedules so they'll have a chance to say, "I can meet then" or "Yes, I can do that."

Action

Create two different calendars for other kinds of learners besides students enrolled in courses. For instance, you could design conflicting calenders for two middle-level managers who must schedule a conference call, or for two club members who are trying to arrange time for committee meeting.

As we have seen in earlier chapters, intonation is extremely important in speaking English. Intonation conveys rather basic information (e.g., that an utterance is a question rather than a statement). However, it also gives more subtle information about a speaker's attitude, such as disbelief, disapproval, or sarcasm. Here is some information on intonation from a text for advanced learners:

Example 10

Review: Question Intonation

In Chapter Three, you saw that your voice goes up at the end of *yes/no* questions, and down at the end of *wh-* questions. Here are some examples:

Did you do anything interesting this week^{end}?

What did you do this week_{end}?

When you hear a *yes/no* question, the speaker expects an answer beginning with *yes* or *no*. When you hear a *wh-* question, the speaker expects a longer, more informative answer.

In casual conversation, a *yes/no* question doesn't always begin with *Do/Does* or *Did:* In using this structure, the speaker is asking for confirmation of what he/she already thinks is true. Here is an example:

You went to the beach this week^{end}?

Adapted from Hartmann and Blass, 2000, p. 116

After modeling and practicing with the whole class, you can have students in pairs use these two different intonation patterns in asking each other questions. They should try to convey clearly whether they are seeking information or confirmation.

All these pronunciation activities (and many more) can help advanced learners sound more natural and be understood. They may never sound like native speakers (and may not want to!), but they can increase their comprehensibility.

6. Speaking in the classroom

At the advanced level, students can do many interesting things with English. In the following extracts, Japanese is the students' first language. The extracts consist of some excerpts from a group discussion in which a woman called Mari and a man called Toshi are peer reviewing an essay by a third student, Nori. He is also present and is listening while they discuss his paper. (These are all pseudonyms.)

These three students are enrolled in a course of English for academic and professional purposes. Nori's essay deals with friendships between American students and international students. In this transcript, two or three periods together in an utterance represent pauses, and (XXX) represents utterances that could not be transcribed with confidence. (These data were collected by Renée Jourdenais and transcribed by Cicely Rude.)

> **Extract 1**
>
> **Toshi:** Mm.
> **Mari:** Yeah. However, I feel his essay just um, how can I say, long? Because um, almost all his... almost all of his paper is um, his experience so if you put uh, (XXX)... how can I say?
> **Toshi:** Leevly...Lively!
> **Mari:** Lively? Yeah. Um, if um, the essay needs more lively parts. Yeah, I think um, yeah but it's very powerful.
> **Toshi:** Yes, powerful.
> **Mari:** Powerful, already.
> **Toshi:** For me his essay seems to be perfect but if I can say something uh, I really want to hear his stance.
> **Mari:** Oh, yeah! I wanna say that.
> **Toshi:** So I really wanted to ask him uh, what will you (XXX) maintain your original stance, accepting American culture in the world.
> **Mari:** Yeah.
> **Toshi:** Because he is ah, he cannot become American. His origin...his originality is Japanese.

> **Mari:** Yeah.
>
> **Toshi:** So, how should I say...I wanted to ask his (XXX). Maybe he will get many, many American culture and many American way of thinking. Then, what will he do? That point is uh, how should I say...If he write down about this point, I wanna (XXX) maybe more strong.
>
> **Mari:** Yeah, I agree. So, if he uh, explains his agreement or disagreement in American culture, yes, it's more uh...if he does, so become more critical and his opinions more...more usable I think. Useful.

In the following extract, Toshi and Mari continue to discuss the essay by Nori, who is sitting with them and listening to their comments. Nori's essay was based both on his own opinions and experiences, as well as on a single article he had read about cultural diversity in the United States.

Extract 2

> **Toshi:** So, did you find out some part you cannot agree his opinion?
>
> **Mari:** Mmm....
>
> **Toshi:** He already write down here, that part you cannot agree.
>
> **Mari:** Oh yes.
>
> **Nori:** Ah, oh, what you said.. the agreement, what you disagree that my opinion people cannot...because of no time.
>
> **Toshi:** I disagree with this. Because American can make a time, if they want. So, of course kind of ah, I'm teasing his article right now because his article looks very perfect.
>
> **Mari:** Yeah, I agree.
>
> **Toshi:** Yeah, so already I understand he is saying but I just disagree.
>
> **Mari:** I have no disagree at this point.
>
> **Toshi:** So, how about this? Connection between (XXX) for international students and cultural diversity. What does it mean connection?
>
> **Mari:** Connection means link...relation.
>
> **Toshi:** Let me explain...connection? Link?
>
> **Nori:** I think, I wrote this essay to you know, this paper as an indicator to develop students' cultural diversity and understanding of cultural diversity to survive in the United States. But you know, the topic of the article was different...it explained just cultural difference, right?
>
> **Toshi:** Yeah.
>
> **Nori:** But my main point is the, some proposal or suggestion to students to survive in the United States. Is it clear for you?
>
> **Mari:** Um, I think uh, regarding international students is a little weak because um, he wrote that his uh, experiences, travel

experience and other experiences he wrote well, just suggest that they make the suggestion point to the students. Weak, weak.

Toshi: *I think ah, he did good job because this article is not so, ah, these essays are not so long so he tried to make many many detailed expression and yeah, I...I think that he did good job but, if I can say something, if he narrow...ah, focus on few example, maybe his message and his suggestion become more specific and more... strong message.*

Mari: *Yeah yeah.*

In the next extract, Nori and Toshi discuss Mari's essay. When they mention a "single source" essay, they are referring to the fact that their essay was based on an assignment to incorporate ideas from an article they had read.

Extract 3

Nori: *Next essay, is Toshi. Oh thank you.*

Mari: *Next is me?*

Nori: *Ah, oh, you. So...certain parts of her article I could agree. I could agree with parts her article because you know, I can understand Japanese and Korean has similar cultures. So mm...the examples are well compared, Korean and Japan, but some of her opinion I cannot agree. For example, in second page...*

Toshi: *Yes, uh huh.*

Nori: *In the past almost all Japanese marriage were arranged, yet it has changed by effect of westernization. Usually make (XXX) usually strong but at the end of sentence, perhaps. I wanted to say 'are you really sure about this?' If you want to say this sentence, if you want to say, make clear this sentence, I can understand if you give me more examples and background information. Of course I can understand because I am Japanese, but I not totally agree with this sentence. Some, third page is 'however in Japan usually the wife has less power than the husband compared to Korea.' I want more background information for this because not all wives weaker than husband. So...hm. I feel I wanted to, I want more information about this. Like something and third page 'In my country remarrying is not welcome by the reason that it's not loyal for' (XXX). I think this is not always. These are I think, I need more background information for these examples. I can understand, I am Japanese, I have background information, I know history, but if you...if the reader is not, they could not understand. They might not.*

Toshi: *Yes, I agree with you, but I also think her single source essay seems to be perfect because Mari's style and Nori's style are* *totally different, but uh, uh, yeah. Seems to be very perfect. However, if can say something to her, I say maybe able to become more specific. I have got a comment. It is a kind of general idea. Everyone can agree. Therefore, if she write her own idea based on her own experience, it can be more specific and more impress...uh yeah, impress. But I think that's a very good essay. Oh yeah, and if she does so she may capture readers' attention more. Then what do you like most about her paper?*

Nori: *Her paper could compare well two cultures. This, is this similarity or is this difference? It was clear for me.*

Toshi: *Yeah, and when she had uh, (XXX) citation, she always used, she always put after author's citation so that was good. Good point. She always tried to explain why. So her style is very good, just I want to, I want her own experience. Her own ideas.*

Nori: *Right, I think so too. These are general ideas, so, as I said, if Mari put in her experience or something like that it would be more clear and easy to understand. So um, her difficult is I really want to know, I really want to hear from her. First page, maybe, 'My home country there are many ways of thinking based on Confus..s.. Con-fu-cian-i-sm (as if sounding it out). It affects Japanese life (XXX).' I want you to explain how that Confucianism affects people in Japanese life more. That's a very curious and interesting part, so I really wanted to hear from her.*

All three of these learners were enrolled in an advanced course in English for academic and professional purposes at a college. Yet their English speaking abilities differ somewhat. Compare the speech of Nori, Toshi, and Mari. Who is the most proficient speaker of English? Who is the least proficient? Why do you think so? Compare your ideas with a classmate or colleague.

In Extract 4, the next part of this discussion, Mari seeks clarification and advice about her writing from Toshi and Nori. Notice the various strategies the three students use to make sure they understand and are understood.

Extract 4

Mari: *Thank you. Ee tou* (a Japanese expression, roughly equivalent to um, uh) *Both of you have um, did you mean my essay is little (XXX) of the author's opinion, right?*

Toshi: *Mm.*

Mari: *Kay. If my article includes same citations, what about if I put more my experience and my idea, my essay become...my essay will have good (XXX) do you think?*

Toshi: *Not only (XXX) but also...I need more information. Why you think this? I think, why, you can use citation from the article to support why you think this.*

Nori: *Ah, I think same thing.*

Mari: *(XXX)*

Toshi: *If Mari do so, maybe such a style will become some message to reader. So I think it's a very good.*

Mari: *(laughs)*

Toshi: *Actually, when we write down, we don't have to worry about message, but if you write down very specifically and a detail and example, such a style will become a, yeah, some message to readers. Surely reader will get some message.*

Mari: *My general idea in this essay is sometimes not clear. You mean...?*

Nori: *Not clear, I mean, when I read this I cannot help stop being down. Is that really? Because I think it's because of 'perhaps' at end of the sentence.*

Mari: *Yeah, perhaps. (laughs) Because before I use 'all' persons, it's confusing. Um, if I put my opinions included background and more, yeah background it is better.*

Nori: *I can, I can get your opinion and your curiosity about the culture, but...if I'm not Japanese maybe I cannot fully understand that curiosity and understand.*

Mari: *Ah. Thank you.*

7. Assessing advanced learners

Assessing the speaking skills of advanced learners should be as direct as possible. That is, within the practical constraints of your situation, speaking tasks should truly involve the students in situations where they must speak English in novel utterances and even deal with unexpected circumstances. Testing learners on their ability to speak English in new contexts will promote positive **washback.** Carefully designed role-plays can be used for this purpose.

Some teachers and learners really like role-plays (both for teaching and for testing), while others don't. How do you feel? Does your stance change if you think of yourself as a language learner, rather than as an English teacher?

There are many reasons to use role-plays in English classes, both as opportunities for speaking and as assessment procedures. But there are also reasons NOT to use role-plays, particularly if students' grades will be influenced by the outcomes. With a classmate or colleague, brainstorm the pro's and con's of using role-plays in assessing the speaking skills of advanced learners. If you are taking a course, compare your list with those of your classmates.

Role-plays are useful for practicing speech in a variety of contexts. What are some situations in which your advanced students (or future students) must use spoken English in an interaction? Are they likely to be talking to strangers, to people they know, or both? Make a list of five or six possible role-play topics for advanced learners. Choose your favorite and write the steps of the role-play for the learners to follow.

Here is an example of a role-play task used in a test designed by Pat Bolger. Part of the test assessed the students' reading comprehension. The reading section included several brief articles about current events that had not really been adequately covered by the press. Bolger was working with enrolled university students at the Monterey Institute of International Studies. These advanced learners were taking graduate courses with native speakers of English and other proficient non-native speakers. They needed to use spoken English to defend their opinions and argue for a position, so he set up this role-play situation to elicit those skills. Notice that the two participants in the role-play are social equals who are quite familiar with each other.

> **Example 11**
>
> Imagine that you are an editor for a major newspaper. You are concerned about presenting the truth to the public.
>
> The stories that you just read [i.e., in the reading comprehension section of the test] have not been published in your newspaper and you think they should be. Unfortunately, your fellow editor and friend of many years, David York, is not so receptive to the stories. He thinks that they are too controversial for the public and are not supported by any data. Moreover, most of the other newspapers have not covered these stories, so why should he?
>
> You feel that these news stories should be covered in one way or another in your newspaper since the public was never really informed of them. So you decide to present your case to David York. Chose one or more of the articles that you feel most comfortable presenting to him and make your case.

Adapted from Bolger, as described in Bailey, 1998, p. 176

Bolger wanted to evaluate the students' speech in terms of how persuasive they were so he adapted a scale from Hughes (1989, pp. 95–96), which emphasizes the speakers' effectiveness of argumentation. This kind of holistic rating scale (see p. 25) is called a **primary trait scoring** system because students are evaluated on the one particular trait characteristic (i.e., the primary trait) which is being emphasized. Here is the scale he used:

Example 12

> ### Holistic Scale for Rating a Speaker's Effectiveness of Argumentation
>
> **7.** Relevant arguments are presented in an interesting way, with main ideas prominently and clearly stated, with completely effective supporting material; arguments are effectively related to the speaker's view.
>
> **6.** Relevant arguments are presented in an interesting way; main ideas are highlighted with effective supporting material, and are well related to the speaker's own views.
>
> **5.** Arguments are well presented with relevant supporting material and an attempt to relate them to the speaker's views.
>
> **4.** Arguments are presented but it may be difficult for the rater to distinguish main ideas from supporting material; main ideas may not be supported; their relevance may be dubious; arguments may not be related to the speaker's views.
>
> **3.** Arguments are presented, but may lack relevance, clarity, consistency, or support; they may not be related to the speaker's views.
>
> **2.** Arguments are inadequately presented and supported; they may be irrelevant; if the speaker's views are presented, they may be difficult to see.
>
> **1.** Some elements of information are present, but the rater is not provided with an argument, or the argument is mainly irrelevant.
>
> **0.** A meaning comes through occasionally but is not relevant.

Adapted from Hughes, 1989, pp. 95-96

Some people feel strongly that role-plays should *not* be used in language assessment because they seem to call on acting ability as well as language proficiency (see, for example, van Lier, 1989). Other people feel that role-plays are ideal for simulating interactions in which learners must use the target language in unpredicted ways. What do you think?

Write a role-play prompt that leads two people to have a discussion in which they hold different points of view. (Choose a topic that is culturally appropriate and relevant for your learners.)

If possible, have two advanced learners perform the role-play, and tape record them as they do. Ask their opinions of the experience.

Afterwards, use the Effectiveness of Argumentation Rating Scale and assign a score to each person's speaking during the role-play.

Finally, ask a colleague or a classmate to evaluate the recorded speech samples using this scale. Discuss the two sets of scores: were your scores totally different, similar, or the same?

Keep in mind that with primary trait scoring, the rating categories should be aligned with the purpose of the communication. For example, consider the speeches produced by learners in the picture-based activity about attracting tourists and getting a contract from a travel agency (see pages 132-133). In that case, the scoring could be based on the convincing descriptions of the area given by the learners. If you are going to draft a primary trait scoring system, first determine the key purpose of the communication. Then write brief descriptions for each rating level that characterize how well that purpose was achieved.

Advanced learners can benefit from feedback on their extemporaneous speeches. Evaluative comments or ratings can come from the teacher or the students' peers.

Example 13

Name _____ Date _____

Oral Presentation Evaluation Sheet

Topic or Title _____

Presenter or Group _____

Did the presenter or group:	lowest	mid		highest
1. make use of eye contact and facial expressions?	1 2	3	4	5
2. have a good opening?	1 2	3	4	5
3. change the pitch and tone of voice?	1 2	3	4	5
4. use interesting and specific language?	1 2	3	4	5
5. use pauses or emphasis on key words?	1 2	3	4	5
6. support ideas with details and examples?	1 2	3	4	5
7. use gestures or action?	1 2	3	4	5
8. use visuals?	1 2	3	4	5
9. speak clearly?	1 2	3	4	5
10. have a good closing?	1 2	3	4	5

For a Reader's Theater or play

	lowest	mid		highest
11. wear costumes or use props?	1 2	3	4	5
12. act so I believed the story?	1 2	3	4	5

Visions: Language, Literature and Content (Assessment Program – Book C)
(McCloskey and Stack, 2004, p. 123)

The learners can also complete self-evaluations. Here is an example of an Oral Presentation Evaluation Sheet, which students can use to rate their classmates' speeches. The following "Speaking Checklist" can be used by individual learners to evaluate their own speeches. The spaces at the bottom allow the students to tailor the form to include particular areas they wish to work on.

Example 14

Name _____ Date _____

Topic _____

Speaking Checklist

Use this checklist to evaluate your speaking.

1. Did I speak too slowly, too quickly, or just right? _____

2. Was the tone of my voice too high, too low, or just right? _____

3. Did I speak loudly enough for the audience to hear me? _____ Yes _____ No

4. Did I produce the correct intonation patterns of sentences? _____ Yes _____ No

5. Did I have a good opening? _____ Yes _____ No

6. Did I look at my audience? _____ Yes _____ No

7. Did I speak with feeling? _____ Yes _____ No

8. Did I support my ideas with facts and examples? _____ Yes _____ No

9. Did I tell the audience how I feel about the topic? _____ Yes _____ No

10. Did I use interesting, specific words? _____ Yes _____ No

11. Did I use visuals to make the speech interesting? _____ Yes _____ No

My Own Criteria

12. _____ _____ Yes _____ No

13. _____ _____ Yes _____ No

14. _____ _____ Yes _____ No

Visions: Language, Literature and Content (Assessment Program – Book C)
(McCloskey and Stack, 2004, p. 125)

8. Conclusion

In this chapter, we have explored the teaching of speaking to advanced students. We began by considering how a simple needs assessment process can help teachers identify key issues for advanced learners. We then discussed three important principles that should inform the teaching of speaking at this level. Next we examined some tasks and materials for teaching speaking to advanced learners including conversations and other interactions, the fluency relay, an advanced picture-based activity, extemporaneous speaking, role-plays, and simulations. We considered some pronunciation issues before examining some excerpts of groupwork interaction among advanced learners. Finally, we considered using role-plays and primary trait scoring to assess advanced students' speaking skills.

Working with advanced learners can be challenging because they already know so much about English and they will often ask difficult questions about complex parts of the language. Continuing to work on the development of their speaking skills can also be frustrating for students with higher proficiency. Many feel that improvement at this level is slower and harder to achieve than it was earlier in their language learning efforts.

On the other hand, teaching speaking to advanced learners can be very rewarding, too. At this level students who continue to enroll in English classes typically have clear goals for improving their English. As a result, they often work hard and have high motivation. Their proficiency is strong enough for them to understand most clear, oral explanations (about grammar, speech acts, vocabulary, pronunciation, and so on). In addition, they can be actively engaged in noticing the gap between their speech and native or other proficient speakers of English.

Further readings

Celce-Murcia, M., D. Brinton, and J. Goodwin. 1996. *Teaching Pronunciation: A Reference for Teachers of English to Speakers of Other Languages.* Cambridge: Cambridge University Press.

> This is an excellent resource for learning more about helping learners improve their pronunciation. It is thorough, yet highly readable.

Wallwork, A. 1997. *Discussions, A - Z (Advanced): A Resource Book of Speaking Activities.* Cambridge: Cambridge University Press.

> This is a very helpful book of discussion topics supported by legally photocopiable visuals and tasks. Topics include issues related to the human body, justice, intelligence, the Zodiac, war, science, and personality, among others. There is also an intermediate version.

Helpful Web site

Supports for Pronunciation Teaching (www.gsu.edu/~esljmm/ss/furtherreading.htm)

> If you have an interest in teaching English pronunciation, John Murphy's Web site is a very good resource.

References

The American Council on the Teaching of Foreign Languages (ACTFL)

Bailey, K.M. 1998. *Learning About Language Assessment: Dilemmas, Decisions, and Directions.* Boston, MA: Heinle & Heinle.

Beck, A. 1983. A Needs Analysis and Flexible Curriculum Plan for Heterogeneous Adult Learners of English as a Second Language. Unpublished masters thesis in TESL. Los Angeles, CA: University of California at Los Angeles.

Byrd, D.R.H. and I.C. Clemente. 2001. *React, Interact: Situations for Communication* (3rd ed.). White Plains, NY: Pearson Education.

Crookall, D. and K. Arai. 1995. *Simulations and Gaming Across Disciplines and Cultures: Isaga at the Watershed.* Thousand Oaks, CA: Sage Publications.

Dörnyei, Z. and S. Thurrell. 1992. *Conversation and Dialogues in Action.* New York, NY: Prentice Hall International English Language Teaching.

Hammerly, H. 1991. *Fluency and Accuracy: Toward Balance in Language Teaching and Learning.* Clevedon, UK: Multilingual Matters, Ltd.

Hartmann, P. and L. Blass. 2000. *Quest: Listening and Speaking in the Academic World, Book 3.* Boston, MA: McGraw-Hill.

Hughes, A. 1989. *Testing for Language Teachers.* Cambridge: Cambridge University Press.

Jones, K. 1982. *Simulations in Language Teaching.* Cambridge: Cambridge University Press.

Krashen, S.D. 1985. *The Input Hypothesis: Issues and Implications.* London: Longman.

Ladousse, G.P. 1987. *Role Play.* Oxford: Oxford University Press.

Matthews, C. and J. Marino. 1990. *Professional Interactions: Oral Communicational Skills in Science, Technology, and Medicine.* Englewood Cliffs, NJ: Prentice Hall Regents.

McCloskey, M.L. and L. Stack. 2004. *Visions: Language, Literature and Content (Assessment Program–Book C).* Boston, MA: Thompson Heinle.

Schmidt, R. and S.N. Frota. 1986. Developing Basic Conversational Ability in a Second Language: A Case Study of an Adult Learner of Portuguese. In R.R. Day (ed.), *Talking to Learn: Conversation in Second Language Acquisition.* Rowley, MA: Newbury House, 237–326.

Shaw, P. 2004. Conversation.

van Lier, L. 1989. Reeling, Writhing, Drawling, Stretching, and Fainting in Coils: Oral Proficiency Interviews as Conversation. *TESOL Quarterly,* 23(3): 489-508.

Chapter **Five**

Key issues in teaching speaking

Goals

At the end of this chapter, you should be able to:

✔ **discuss** the use of the learners' first language in the speaking classroom.

✔ **explain** some strategies for managing speaking turns in classes.

✔ **describe** ways of teaching speaking with learners who have reflective and/or impulsive learning styles.

✔ **discuss** options for responding to students' oral errors during speaking classes.

✔ **identify** some challenges of teaching speaking in large classes.

✔ **develop** some strategies for managing groupwork and pairwork in large classes.

✔ **understand** some challenges of teaching speaking in "multi-level" classes.

✔ **recognize** the potential value of pronunciation software, chat rooms, corpora, and Web sites in helping students improve their speaking skills.

1. Introduction

In this chapter, we will consider several key issues about teaching speaking. These are matters of concern for most teachers, but they can be particularly challenging for new teachers. We will begin with a discussion of using the students' first language in the ESL/EFL classroom. We will also look at students' participation patterns, including their reticence to speak and the tendency for some learners to dominate during speaking activities. Then we will consider teaching speaking in large and/or **multi-level classes.** Finally, we will briefly consider some technological tools for improving students' speaking and pronunciation.

2. Students' first-language use in the English speaking class

The learners' first language is also referred to as their native language, mother tongue, or just the "L1." What is the appropriate role of the students' first language in a speaking class? There are many possible answers to this question and they vary quite a bit, depending on whether you are teaching in an **ESL** or an **EFL** situation. (Some institutions actually have regulations governing the use of the learners' L1, so you should ask what the rules are, if you are new to a school.)

In an ESL context, the students in any one class may have many different native languages. This diversity is an advantage, in some regards, since the learners will probably need to use English to communicate with one another (and with you, if you don't speak their languages). There is also the chance you teach ESL in a neighborhood where there are high concentrations of people who share a common first language. In this case it's only natural that students would use that language regularly to communicate with one another.

In an EFL situation, however, typically all or most of the students speak the same native language. Having a shared language means the students can talk with each other without using English. Of course, it is easier to communicate in a language we know well than in one we are learning. As a result, the need to communicate in their first language may seem especially strong to beginning learners, false beginners, and lower intermediate students.

Some language teachers ban the use of the students' L1 in their speaking classes. This policy may not be very realistic, and it could make the students feel quite uncomfortable. Making such a rule could suggest that you do not value their mother tongue. It can also be very frustrating for lower-level adult students not to be able to express themselves. Sometimes they want to share an idea with a classmate in their common first language to see how to express the concept in English. They may use their mother tongue to ask for help or clarification about classwork. Sometimes they speak their native language to help a classmate. As the teacher, you must decide what you think about L1 use in the English class, based on your students' proficiency levels, program policy, and your course goals.

Reflection

When you have taken a foreign language class, did the teacher allow the students to speak in their mother tongue? As a language learner, would you want to use your L1 in class or not? Does your answer change if you think of yourself as a beginning student? An intermediate? And an advanced speaker?

My own preference as a teacher is not to discourage the students from using their first language up to a point, but to build their confidence in using English. I also try to build their willingness to take risks. For example, when I would ask a question in English, my EFL university students in Hong Kong would typically turn to a classmate and whisper quickly in Cantonese before answering the question in English. This behavior puzzled me because I was sure they had understood my question.

Finally, I asked one of the students why they consulted with one another before answering. She told me they checked with each other to make sure they had the correct answer before responding. This idea made sense because they had all come through a secondary school system in which accuracy was emphasized and oral errors were quickly (and sometimes harshly) corrected. So rather than fighting the students' preference, I decided to build in an intentional step in which students talked briefly with one another, and "buzz with a buddy" became a regular feature of our classes. When setting up a speaking task or asking for opinions or answers, I would tell the students to "buzz with a buddy," to make sure they and their classmates understood the task or question, knew the answers, etc. They could buzz in Cantonese if they wanted to before responding publicly in English.

What surprised me about this "buzz with a buddy" strategy was that pretty soon, as the students began to believe that it was okay to make mistakes when speaking English, the amount of Cantonese used in our class decreased. After a while when they'd "buzz with a buddy," their quick conversations were mostly in English.

Let's look at an interaction where learners use their common L1 to help a classmate. Here is a brief sample of classroom talk from an adult beginning level ESL class in California. All of the students are native speakers of Spanish, and they are all undocumented aliens. (That is, they are working in the country illegally.) They had listened to an audiotape about the weather and road conditions. Student 1, whose pseudonym is Maria, was the least proficient student. The researcher's microphone was on the table, in plain view of the students. In the transcript below, when the teacher makes a joke about the FBI (the U.S. Federal Bureau of Investigation) and the microphone, he is acknowledging, within the safety of the shared culture of the classroom, that these students are in the country illegally. The excerpt begins with the teacher saying the word *mud*, which was an important idea in the recorded message about road conditions.

Extract 1

T: Mud.

S1: What you mean?

T: Oh, OK. OK. You know what dirt is.

S2: Mmhmm (affirmative).

S3: Dirt.

T: OK. When it rains, the dirt turns into mud.

S2: Lodo.

T: Wet.

S3: Lodo.
S4: Lodo.

T: Lodo?

S3: Yeah.

S4: Lodo.

T: MUDDY (in a deep voice). M-U-D-D-Y. MUDDY. (Everyone laughs a lot.) DIRTY D-I-R-T-Y. DIRTY. (Everyone laughs.) This is the FBI (he laughs). OK, that's what mud is. How do you say it, lodo?

S4: Lodo.

T: Lodo.

S3: Lodo.

T: Loco lodo. OK. What is a camper, Maria?

S1: Like a van with a bed, kitchen, and bathroom.

These data were collected and transcribed by Mandy Dealand; reprinted from Allwright and Bailey, 1991, p. 143.

Several interesting things happen in this brief interaction. First, the teacher told me that Maria (S1) was the quietest and least proficient student in class. He said she seldom asked questions, but here she asks, "What you mean?" The teacher chose <u>not</u> to correct her grammar error ("What <u>do</u> you mean?"). Instead, he responded by explaining that mixing dirt and water produces mud. ("You know what dirt is…. OK. When it rains, the dirt turns into mud.") Meanwhile, three other students then said *lodo,* the Spanish word for *mud.* The teacher spelled the words *dirty* and *muddy* for the class in the middle of joking about the FBI eavesdropping on their classroom interaction through the researcher's tape recorder. The other students appeared to be helping S1 to understand the word *mud* by providing the Spanish word. At the end of the episode, the teacher joked about "loco lodo" (crazy mud) and the lesson moved on.

Reflection

What do you think of this teacher's use of joking? What roles can humor play in a language class—and specifically in a speaking class?

There are some benefits of L1 use in language classes. For example, research has shown that learners use their first language to manage tasks in the target language by getting acquainted with the texts, pictures, or manipulables to be used in the tasks (Swain and Lapkin, 2000). They also use it to clarify their understanding of the task and to set their goals (Brooks and Donato, 1994). Research in Australia identified four functions of L1 use in the language classroom (see also McCarthy and Walsh, 2003, pp. 178–182):

1. *task management:* discussion about how the task should be completed or how the written text should be constructed
2. *task clarification:* discussion about the meaning of the task…instructions
3. *vocabulary and meaning:* discussions about lexical choice and definitions of words
4. *grammar:* deliberations about grammatical points

(Storch and Wigglesworth, 2003, p. 763)

In this study, the learners said that using their native language helped them "to provide each other with difficult vocabulary and explanations of grammar, particularly when they did not have the required metalanguage" (Storch and Wigglesworth, 2003, p. 765). **Metalanguage** is language used to talk about language. When we refer to grammar categories such as *subject, verb,* and *direct object,* we are using metalanguage.

Action

Look back at the four Extracts in Chapter 4—the transcripts of three advanced learners of English involved groupwork. The students shared a common L1 (Japanese) and were not closely supervised by the teacher. Locate all instances of their use of Japanese. What do you conclude?

3. Reticence and dominance in speaking activities

A great deal of research has shown that students are often hesitant and anxious about speaking the target language in class. In fact, researchers have studied **language classroom anxiety**. This term refers to the situationally triggered anxiousness that learners experience when they try to interact in the target language during lessons.

Reflection

Think about a time when you were learning a new language, when you were still at the lower levels of your speaking ability. Did you feel uncomfortable about speaking that language initially? If so, what made you feel uncomfortable? List three things that made you feel anxious.

What can we, as teachers, do to help our learners overcome their anxiety and take advantage of opportunities to practice speaking? A group of secondary school EFL teachers in Hong Kong studied their own English classes (Tsui, 1996). They first gathered data through a variety of means (videotaping, audiorecording, surveying the students) and examined the data to see what they could learn about their students' oral participation in English. As a result, they found some predictable and some unpredictable reasons for their students' reticence to speak English. On examining their data, the teachers learned the students' reticence could be attributed to five factors: (1) the students' low English proficiency; (2) the students' fear of mistakes and the derision they thought they would face as a result; (3) the teachers' intolerance of silence; (4) the teachers' uneven allocation of turns; and (5) incomprehensible input from the teachers. The first two results were predictable, but the teachers were surprised by the other three. It seems the teachers themselves were creating conditions that contributed to the students' reticence.

These teachers then came up with the following strategies for dealing with the students' reticence. First, they lengthened their **wait-time** and improved their questioning techniques. They tried to accept a variety of answers and build in peer support and groupwork. They also made an attempt to focus on content. Finally, they worked at establishing good relationships in their classes (Tsui, 1996, pp. 148–164). Their research suggests that teachers can take steps to reduce learners' anxiety and encourage them to speak more in class.

The opposite problem of the reticent learner in a speaking class is the person who tends to dominate classroom interaction. This student may speak a great deal because of personality traits, cultural issues, proficiency, or any combination of these factors. Whatever the reason, it is not uncommon to find a few learners who seem to get more than their "fair share" of the talk time. Here is some good advice for both kinds of learners from a popular textbook:

▌Example 1

Taking Turns

When you speak in a group, it's important to take turns. If you like to talk, make sure that you give the quieter group members a chance to speak. You can help them by asking them for their opinions. If you don't like to talk, force yourself to make at least one comment. If you are shy, sometimes it helps to write down your ideas first and then say them.

Quest: Listening and Speaking in the Academic World, Book One (Hartmann and Blass, 2000, p. 254)

Extract 2 is from a lower intermediate evening class of adult ESL learners in Los Angeles. The transcript is an attempt to represent verbal interaction as it actually happened. The following excerpt is from a vocabulary lesson. The vocabulary items the teacher is focusing on are *claim* and *get to* (as in getting someone to do something). The vocabulary came from a reading passage about air pollution. One student (S2 in Extract 2), a man from Russia whose pseudonym is Igor, got interested in the topic of air pollution. In fact, it seems from the transcript that he wanted to talk about air pollution issues more than about the vocabulary items.

The extract uses a variety of conventions to represent spoken language in writing. The boldface print (for instance, when the teacher says "That would be **ex**claim") represents heavy contrastive stress on the word (*exclaim* versus *claim*). Indented lines indicate **turn overlaps** (two people speaking at the same time). For example, in lines 8 and 9, you'll see that Igor says "Yeah" while the teacher is saying "the pollution problem." X's represent speech that was too indistinct to transcribe well. As you read this excerpt, try to determine how Igor gets so many turns.

Extract 2

T: Yeah. Or to make an accusation. OK. You say he he did, he killed that man, OK. You claim, that, but you, if you can't prove it, it's only a claim. Yeah?

S2: It's to say something louder?

T: No. That would be **ex**claim. To, to, make shout, say something loud, it's exclaim.

S2: He claims...

T: Yeah.

S2: I think they'd better produce electric machine for car to use.

T: For, for to end the pollution problem?

S2:   Yeah.

S2: Yeah.

T: Yeah. OK. What does this mean? 'Get to'? Uh.

Ss: XXX

Originally from Allwright, 1980; reprinted from Allwright and Bailey, 1991, p. 125

Here the teacher first answers Igor's question about saying something louder. Next she clarifies that his idea about producing electric machines is related to air pollution. Finally, she tries to move the class on to a discussion of *get to*, the next item on the vocabulary list.

The teacher of this class said that Igor often talked more than the other students and got more than his "fair share" of the speaking turns in class. Look at Extract 3, the next segment of transcript from this lesson. How does Igor get turns? How many questions does the teacher ask Igor in this second segment of the transcript?

Extract 3

T: OK. It says the group has been trying to get the government, the city government, to help uhm draw special lanes, lanes like this (draws on board) *on the street. OK. These are for cars. These are for bikes...* (pointing to the blackboard).

S2: You know, in Moscow they reproduce all all cab.

T: Uhm?

S2: They reproduced all cabs XXX.

T: They produce?

S2: **Re**produce.

T: D'you mean uh they they use old cabs, old taxis?

S2: No, no, no, they reproduced all A-L-L cabs.

T: All the cabs?

S2: Yeah, all the cabs for electric electric, you know electric (points to the electric light).

T: Cab. Oh, you mean they made the cabs in down in downtown areas uh uh use electric uh motors?

S2: Yeah, no downtown, all cabs in Moscow.

T: Where?

S2: In Moscow.

T: Oh. And it's successful?

S2: Yeah.

T: OK. Uhm. Just a second, Igor. Let's what does this mean? If you get someone to do something. Uhm.

Originally from Allwright, 1980; reprinted from Allwright and Bailey, 1991, pp. 125–126

If you count you will see that the teacher asks Igor six questions, and he responds to all six of them. So one way to look at the teacher's view that Igor was taking too many turns is that the teacher herself was giving him too many turns!

Reflection

What can you do as the teacher if someone seems to dominate the class discussions? If you think the behavior is negative, you can try to adjust the turn distribution system in your class. Think of three things this teacher could have done to get other learners involved in the discussion with Igor. Share your ideas with a classmate or colleague.

The challenge in working with students who tend to dominate classroom interaction is to get them to manage their turn-taking behavior without discouraging them from participating. Here are some techniques you can use to control the speaking turns in your lessons:

- Put every student's names on an index card. Shuffle the cards and call on the students randomly.
- Have a student who has finished speaking choose the next person to talk.
- When several students are bidding for turns, tell them the sequence in which they will speak: "Okay, I see several raised hands. Let's hear first from Ali, then Mohammed, and then Amel."
- Give the most talkative students special, non-talking responsibilities (scorekeeper, recording secretary or notetaker, timekeeper, etc.).
- Talk to the dominating students individually and explain to them that everyone needs a chance to talk.

Figure 1 shows that classroom turns can either be initiated by a student or by the teacher. If a student seeks, takes, or makes an opportunity to talk in class, it is called a **self-initiated turn**. The student can either bid for turns (e.g., by raising his hand, by saying, "excuse me," or by taking a sharp inbreath, indicating a desire to speak) or take an unbidden turn by simply speaking out. In other words, **bidding for turns** is done both verbally and non-verbally.

Speaking turns are also distributed by the teacher initiating the turn-taking. Teachers initiate students' turns either by directly nominating an individual to speak or by posing a question or task to the class in general. Again, direct and general nominations for turns can both be done verbally and non-verbally.

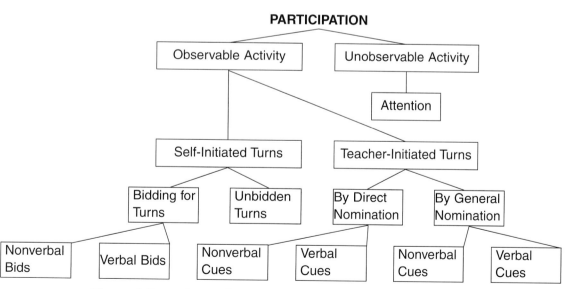

Figure 1 Some factors in observable participation in classrooms (Allwright and Bailey, 1991, p. 128)

Look back at Extracts 2 and 3 on pages 165 and 166, the entire transcript of the teacher interacting with Igor. How many self-initiated turns does Igor take? How many teacher-initiated turns is he given? Compare your tabulations with those of a colleague or classmate.

Ironically, one student dominating a class discussion seems to be most problematic in **"teacher-fronted" lessons**. This phrase refers to classes in which the teacher manages the turn taking, nominates most of the topics, and generally controls the discourse, often from the front of the classroom. You can disrupt this teacher-fronted pattern by using groupwork, pairwork, or individual work on a regular basis. For instance, you can put two or more vocal students in a group together to accomplish a task. As an alternative, you can give the students a groupwork task and appoint a typically quiet learner to represent each group and report to the whole class afterwards. That way you can make sure the quieter students get a chance to talk.

In open discussions or report-back sessions after groupwork, you can also have the student who is speaking select the next person to speak. They can either do this by naming the next person, or if you are working with a calm, well-behaved group of adults, tossing a ping-pong or tennis ball to the person who'll speak next can be a novel way of allocating turns.

It is often a good idea to maintain an element of unpredictability in the turn distribution process. If you simply go down the rows of students' desks, or call on students in sequence along the tables in the classroom (for instance in conducting a workbook activity), students often predict what task or question will be theirs. As a result, they may focus only on that issue, not listening to their classmates or preparing to respond to any other questions or comments.

In Chapter 4 we saw several excerpts of speech from the groupwork discussions of Nori, Mari, and Toshi, three native speakers of Japanese who were advanced learners of English. At the end of the group time, the teacher commented to these three students about their interaction during the groupwork. Their conversation is presented in Extract 4:

Extract 4

Instructor: *Are you guys done? Are you finished? Or not yet?*

Nori: *We're finished.*

Instructor: *'Cause I have to say while I was listening to you guys talk it was so nice to hear, you know? Because a lot of times in class I don't hear your voices and you guys are really bright and you have all of these great ideas and, you know?*

Speak up, because you have really good things to say, you know? How do you feel about in class, speaking up? How does it make you feel?

Nori: *Sometimes I feel I don't need to speak because other guy speaks.*

All: (much laughter)

Instructor: *OK, yeah.*

What does Nori's comment suggest to you as a teacher? Is it the teacher's responsibility to get all the students to speak? If so, how would you like to achieve this goal?

Some teachers "reward" classroom participation (or penalize the lack of it) by giving grades or points for speaking in class. This practice is controversial and could even heighten the problem for students who are anxious about speaking in a foreign language. It could be argued that students have a right not to talk in class, and that it is the learners themselves who should choose if and when to speak. This issue is related to the concept of learning styles.

4. Learning styles in the speaking class

In any speaking class, your students may be very different from one another in terms of how they participate. Some interactional differences are due to personality factors (such as being shy or having an outgoing nature). Others may stem from cultural differences (e.g., some cultures value silence more than others). Still other differences may come from the students' learning styles.

Learning styles are "the way we learn things in general" (Brown, 1994, p. 105). They are "natural, habitual, and preferred ways of absorbing, processing and retaining new information and skills" (Kinsella, 1995, p. 171). Learning styles are relatively stable (though not unchangeable). For example, some students are visual learners who benefit from seeing charts, diagrams, and models. Others are kinesthetic learners, who prefer physical activities for learning new material or skills. (See Christison, 2003, for a helpful discussion of learning styles.)

In Australia, Willing identified four kinds of prevalent styles among adult learners of English. Concrete learners enjoyed using games, films, and cassettes. They like talking in pairs and practicing English outside of class, while analytic learners prefer working alone, reading, and studying grammar. Communicative learners like talking to friends in English, listening to native speakers, and learning through conversation. In contrast, authority-oriented learners want to learn by reading, to write everything in their notebooks, to have their own textbooks, and to have the teacher explain new concepts. (For more detailed information about these four types of learning styles, see Willing, 1987, and Nunan, 2005.)

Reflection

Think about these four learning styles: concrete, analytical, communicative, and authority-oriented. When you are learning a foreign language, does one of these labels describe your preferred learning style? Imagine teaching an English lesson based on conversations among pairs of students. How do you think each type of learner would feel during a speaking lesson?

One learning style issue that influences learners' speaking in class is the contrast between reflectivity and impulsivity. **Reflective learners** prefer to think about their answers or comments before speaking in class. They are generally cautious, while **impulsive learners** tend to be more impetuous and may take a gamble. They may respond immediately, often before they've thought through their ideas completely. So in an English speaking class, impulsive learners are typically those who will speak out quickly, perhaps without much concern for accuracy. Reflective learners, on the other hand, will want to think through what they have to say before speaking out in class (Brown, 1994, pp. 113–114).

Reflection

Think about yourself as a language learner. In class are you more of an impulsive learner or more reflective when you speak a second or foreign language?

The reflectivity-impulsivity dimension is one we language teachers should be aware of. Brown says, "teachers tend to judge mistakes too harshly, especially in the case of a learner with an impulsive style who may be more willing than a reflective person to gamble at a correct answer" (1994, p. 113).

Perhaps Igor (in Extracts 2 and 3) is an example of an impulsive student, and Maria (in Extract 1) may be more reflective. Brown adds that teachers must be patient with more reflective learners, who may need more time to produce utterances during speaking classes.

As teachers, we should not assume that students who don't talk much in class are not participating. Some learners prefer to listen more than speak. Others speak very quietly—almost privately. For example, I once participated in research on classroom turn-taking in which stereo recording microphones were hung above the students' heads. When the research team transcribed one lesson, we found that a learner we called "Chuck" talked more than anyone else. The teacher thought we had labeled the transcripts wrong, because in her experience, Chuck rarely spoke in class. When we played the tape for her, she was very surprised because she could clearly hear Chuck talking a great deal—in fact, almost constantly throughout the lesson. It turned out that Chuck had been sitting directly under the sensitive microphone, which recorded all his quiet talk. The teacher had thought he was not participating—maybe not even paying attention—when, in fact, he was actively engaged in the lesson. He was talking quietly to himself, rather than publicly to his classmates or the teacher.

We should also remember that just because students are quiet, it doesn't necessarily mean they are not participating on some level. Look back at Figure 1 on page 167, at the box under "unobservable activity"—the box labeled "attention." How can we as teachers tell when quiet students are participating in class? Sometimes we can watch their eye movements and head nodding. At other times detecting attention is subtler. For instance, in Extract 1 about *mud*, we can tell that Maria is paying attention, even though she doesn't speak after her first question, because she responds immediately and quickly to the teacher's follow-up question about campers.

Action

If possible, observe an English class. For two minutes focus on a learner who is very quiet, but seems to be involved in the lesson. Make a list of all the observable manifestations of attention that you notice.

With a little structure, both the reflective and the impulsive learners in your classes can use speaking opportunities to their advantage. The key is to not only help both groups use their strengths, but also build on their weaknesses. Before the actual speaking part of an activity you can sometimes have the individual learners write down what they would like to say before they speak. This added step gives the reflective learners time to plan what they want to say, and the impulsive learners time to focus on the accuracy of their responses. Or you can have learners turn to someone next to them and quietly say their answers to their partner before speaking to the entire class. This "buzz with a buddy" step gives reflective learners validation and confidence, and it may give the impulsive learners feedback about their accuracy.

Another technique for balancing reflective and impulsive learners' oral participation is to build in an extended quiet writing step before having a general discussion. For instance, with intermediate English students, you can use an activity in which each student must make two or three suggestions. The suggestions they make would be related to recent lessons, readings, discussions, and so on (for instance, two suggestions about recycling in your town, or for saving money, or for making new friends, or for improving one's test scores).

5. Responding to oral errors

When ESL and EFL learners make errors in their speaking, it can be a potential crisis point for students and teachers alike. Learners' oral errors present a dual dilemma for you as the teacher. First, you must decide whether or not to respond to an error and treat it in some way. Second, if some kind of response is needed, who should do it, and how should it be done?

Reflection

Think of a time when you were learning a new language. Did you always want someone to correct you if you made an error when you were speaking? Why or why not? Does your answer to these questions change depending on whether it was a mistake in grammar, vocabulary, or pronunciation?

Is it really necessary to react to every error a learner makes when speaking English? Research has shown that teachers react to errors more often than non-teachers do. In addition, non-native speaking teachers react more often than native-speaking teachers. These findings suggest that teachers—especially non-native teachers—may be more sensitive to errors than other people.

In fact, there are some good reasons *not* to react to learners' oral errors. We don't want to discourage students who are trying to communicate their ideas and feelings and in fact, people often get their point across even when they make mistakes. In addition, research suggests that correcting grammar points which are too advanced for the learners' current level of linguistic development probably doesn't result in learning anyway.

Who should treat learners' errors? Oddly enough, students may learn more if they themselves correct problems in their speech. If the teacher simply supplies the correct form, the learner may not recall and internalize that form—especially during the pressure of communicating during an on-going conversation. On the other hand, if the learner has to work a bit at producing the correct form, doing so may be memorable, and could promote actual learning (in addition to sustaining the conversation).

Look back to Extracts 2 and 3 above (pp. 165–166). Underline each error in Igor's speech. Compare the errors you marked with those identified by a classmate or a colleague.

Next, look to see whether or not the teacher responded to those errors in some way. If she did respond, how did she choose to treat the error? With your colleague or classmate, brainstorm some ideas for alternative ways of responding.

There are many ways teachers can help students correct their own speaking errors. For instance, if a learner says, "I go to the movies yesterday," you can point backward over your shoulder to indicate that past tense is needed. You can also get the student to repeat the utterance and just raise your hand in a gentle cautioning movement, palm outward, at the point where he makes an error. Giving a simple hint may allow the learner to work out the problem on his own.

There are also times when peer correction can be very effective—especially if it is done in a positive, supportive way. If a learner is having trouble with an utterance, a classmate can often coach him and provide a missing word or structure. Be sure to return to the original speaker if you elicit peer correction, so that he can repeat the corrected form aloud. The point is not to embarrass the students or set up a competitive environment. Rather it is to increase student participation and support.

Another issue is *when* to treat learners' speaking errors. Sometimes it is best to make a note about learners' errors and return to them later. You can respond to errors immediately, or you can wait until the student has finished speaking. Or you can save some time at the end of the lesson to deal with errors that arose during speaking practice. You can also collect examples of learners' errors and use them as the focal point of future lessons.

In general, the practice in **Communicative Language Teaching** is not to interrupt a learner to react to an error if he is communicating his message successfully even with the error. Instead, teachers using this approach typically focus on oral errors if they disrupt communication. Another widely accepted strategy is only to treat those errors in structure, vocabulary, pronunciation, or speech acts that have already been covered in previous lessons. Another idea is to separate initially lessons focused on accuracy from those focused on fluency, and not to deal with errors during fluency practice. Whatever your choice may be, it is important not to treat errors in a punitive fashion, or to belittle the students when they are working hard to communicate in a new language.

Turn back to Extracts 1, 2, 3, and 4 in Chapter 4 (see pp. 146–150). Underline or highlight errors the learners make during their groupwork discussions. Is there any evidence that any of these errors impeded communication? Next, choose one or two errors that were made during those discussions. If you were the teacher and had overheard these utterances, would you (a) correct the errors immediately, (b) wait until the student had finished speaking and then respond, or (c) make a note of the errors and treat them in a future lesson? Explain your choice to a classmate or colleague.

6. Speaking activities in large classes

One of the most challenging situations is teaching speaking in large classes. It is not unusual in many parts of the world to have forty or fifty students in one room, and to teach several large groups every day. Shamim (1996) wrote about classes of 45 to more than 100 students in Pakistan. Nunan (2005, p. 158) states that classes of 30 to 130 occur in many parts of the world. LoCastro reports that, "language education in developing countries is typically carried out in classrooms with 150–300 learners and sometimes more" (2001, p. 494). (See also Sarwar, 2001.)

LoCastro (2001) studied teachers' views of the problems involved in teaching large classes. Several of these are directly related to teaching speaking (pp. 494–495). Compared to small classes, teachers with large classes may experience the following:

- more difficulties in carrying out speaking, reading, and writing tasks
- difficulties in monitoring work and giving feedback
- problems with individualizing work
- difficulties in setting up communicative tasks
- tendency to avoid activities that are demanding to implement
- pairwork and groupwork often cumbersome to execute
- high noise level, affecting neighboring classes
- difficulties in attending to all students during class time
- more acute discipline problems
- crowd phenomenon: students not listening to teacher and other students

These issues do present challenges in speaking classes with large numbers of students, but the challenges are not insurmountable. Depending on your local constraints and resources, you will be able to deal with some of these concerns.

Action

Choose three of the points in this bulleted list that seem particularly challenging to you. Talk to two or three experienced teachers about their strategies for dealing with these issues.

What can we, as teachers, do if we are faced with these issues (or think we might be)? Here are a few strategies for dealing with some of these concerns:

Issue(s)	Strategy
Difficulties in monitoring work and giving feedback	Set up a clear system for self-checking and/or peer-review of homework and in-class exercises.
Problems with individualizing work	Design a simple process of gathering students' ideas. For example, give out strips of paper at the end of a week that say, "The next thing I want to work on is _____."
Difficulties in setting up communicative tasks; pairwork and groupwork often cumbersome to execute	Establish routines for groupwork and pairwork. Make sure learners understand the value of groupwork and pairwork.
Noise level is high, affecting neighboring classes	Talk to neighboring teachers. Explain that speaking classes entail a certain amount of noise. Talk to class members about keeping their voices low. Conduct some pairwork or groupwork activities in "whisper mode."
Difficulties in attending to all students during class time	Decide what "attending to students" means. If you cannot spend much time during class with all the students, try to establish another way of connecting. For instance, arrive early and greet every student as he or she enters the room.

Figure 2 Some issues and strategies for teaching large classes

Of course, these strategies are not foolproof, and there are probably many other ways to deal with these challenges. Wherever you are teaching (or hope to teach), if you are not a member of that particular culture, be sure to ask local teachers about what activities are or are not acceptable in that context.

Action

Choose two or three issues from the bulleted list (p. 174) and brainstorm other possible solutions with a classmate or colleague. Share your solutions with the class or work with some colleagues.

There are two key issues to keep in mind when teaching speaking to large classes. The first is for us to get past the idea that as teachers we should be interacting with one learner at a time, while the others wait and listen. Many opportunities for student talk can develop when we change the usual control patterns that dominate teacher-fronted classroom interaction. Second, establishing set routines for doing groupwork and pairwork can help you with the classroom management and provide students with many more opportunities to talk.

Sometimes having the students speak in unison can be useful. **Choral repetition** was a regular practice in the **Audiolingual Method** when teachers were trying to instill good speaking habits in the students. Choral repetition as a procedure fell out of favor when audiolingualism began to wane. It doesn't allow for creative language use, since the students are just repeating what the teacher said. However, there are times when having the group speak in unison can be very helpful, for instance, in learning the stress, pitch and intonation contours of English utterances. In addition, I have noticed that reticent or less confident learners sometimes seem to feel "safe" during moments of choral repetition.

One useful technique you can use in choral repetition practice is called the **backward build-up.** (This technique is also called "back-chaining.") If you say a long sentence for the students to repeat, they may forget parts of it and falter. But if you start at the end and gradually add phrases, they will be able to recall and reproduce the utterance. For example, consider the sentence, "Mei-ling rode the bus to her job every morning." In a backward build-up, the choral repetition would look something like this:

Extract 5

T: Every morning

Ss: Every morning

T: To her job

Ss: *To her job*

T: *To her job every morning*

Ss: *To her job every morning*

T: *Rode the bus*

Ss: *Rode the bus*

T: *Rode the bus to her job*

Ss: *Rode the bus to her job*

T: *Rode the bus to her job every morning*

Ss: *Rode the bus to her job every morning*

T: *Mei-ling rode the bus.*

Ss: *Mei-ling rode the bus.*

T: *Mei-ling rode the bus to her job every morning.*

Ss: *Mei-ling rode the bus to her job every morning.*

The backward build-up technique is useful for introducing a long sentence and teaching the class the intonation curves of an utterance. Providing this kind of guidance and structure can keep learners from getting confused. In my experience, it is often when students are confused that an activity gets off track. Those learners who are lost may ask their classmates for guidance (which is in general a positive step, although it generates more noise in a crowded classroom). Some learners may ask the teacher for clarification, but while the teacher tries to explain to them, other learners can get bored.

Many teachers–especially new teachers–worry about losing control of the class during speaking activities. They fear that the students will get off task, or start speaking only in their first language, or make mistakes speaking English. It's true that any of these things could happen, but you can help prevent these problems by using clear, systematic procedures for structuring groupwork and pairwork.

For example, you can start getting students used to groupwork and pairwork without a great deal of confusion by having them work with the people seated right near them. Later, when they are accustomed to getting into pairs and quickly starting to work, you can have them number off around the room (1-2-3-4, 1-2-3-4) and have each person with the number 1 pair with someone who is a 3, while the 2's and the 4's pair up.

If there is physical space for the students to move around, you can also have each person draw a slip of colored paper or a number from a box. If you have a class of 40 people, for instance, make four slips with 1, four with 2, four with 3, and so on, up to four with the number 10. Students then get into groups of four depending on the number they draw.

One important way to manage groupwork is to give clear instructions before putting the students into groups. There are several ways to do this.

- Read the instructions aloud, step by step, or have a student with a loud, clear voice read them aloud.
- Write the instructions in short, clear imperative sentences that list the steps the students are to follow.
- After the instructions have been read aloud, call on a student to repeat or paraphrase them loudly for the class. If he leaves anything out or gets something muddled, ask another student to add to what he has said. (If you do this regularly, the learners will soon see that they must pay attention to the instructions.)
- Print the instructions for the task on colored slips of paper. (If you use different colors for the various components of a jigsaw task, for instance, the color of the paper can be the way students find their groups.)
- Model the activity for the students.
- Tell the students explicitly what they need to take with them (pens, pencils, their textbooks) before they move into their groups.
- Post a public copy of the instructions on the board or the overhead transparency projector so everyone can see them.

Action

With a classmate or colleague, brainstorm other strategies for managing groupwork. If possible, observe two or three experienced teachers using groupwork or pairwork. Find out what techniques they use.

7. Multi-level speaking classes

Another challenging context is teaching speaking in multi-level classes. Unless you are teaching true beginning level students, every class will have some variation, but many groups have widely different proficiency levels in one class. Why is this so?

Some programs don't use **placement tests,** and students enter classes based on factors other than their language level. For instance, in adult school programs in the U.S., it is not uncommon for learners to attend classes that are convenient for their work schedules. In EFL conversation courses, learners often choose to attend a particular class because their friends do (i.e., for the social value of the class), and not necessarily because it's the appropriate level for them.

Some programs may use placement tests that don't evaluate the students' speaking ability. Some learners score well on grammar, vocabulary, and reading tests, but their speaking skills may be less developed. Other students who have stronger speaking skills may not be very good in grammar, so they will score lower on grammar oriented placement tests.

Another circumstance that leads to multi-level classes occurs when new students are put into classes on the basis of their placement test scores, while continuing students advance through the curriculum on the basis of their work in the class. In a study of university students in California, Brown (1980) found that learners who started out in a lower intermediate class, then progressed to an intermediate class and then to an upper-intermediate class, consistently scored lower than students who placed directly into the intermediate or upper-intermediate class. In other words, even though the learners in Brown's study worked hard and passed their courses, those students who came through the system didn't seem to catch up with those who were placed directly into the more advanced class.

In speaking classes with students at various levels, the less proficient learners may feel intimidated by their more advanced classmates. On the other hand, the more proficient learners may feel that the other students slow them down. However, with some initiative you can prepare speaking activities that will engage all the learners.

Action

If possible, ask two or three experienced teachers how they deal with speaking activities in multi-level classes.

When you are working with multi-level classes it is helpful to think about each learner's strengths. Some students may be more fluent, while others may be more accurate. Some have creative ideas but may not be able to express them well in English. Some have academic strengths, while others have more varied and interesting life experiences. If you as the teacher publicly recognize and reinforce the various learners' talents and strengths, your students will also respect each other's contributions.

In groupwork situations, you can assign roles to different students, or have them choose their management responsibilities. For example, it is often helpful to have a timekeeper, a note-taker, and someone who will report back to the entire class at the end of the groupwork. Assigning different roles to all of the students over time can help you encourage the quieter students, distribute talking turns, and provide opportunities for balanced interaction.

8. Technology and teaching speaking

There are many ways that teachers can use technology to teach speaking and pronunciation. These include familiar technological resources, such as audio and videorecorders, but computer technology now offers many possibilities as well. These options consist of pronunciation software, vocal message exchanges, chat rooms, corpora, concordancing programs, the Internet, and language teaching Web sites.

Pronunciation software can be very helpful to individual learners and classes (Murphy, 2003). Some programs allow students to listen to a model utterance, repeat the utterance, and see a visual comparison of their speech with the model. The visual image can help learners match their pitch and intonation contours with those of the model. (See, for example, Moholt's 1988 report about using computer programs to improve Chinese learners' English pronunciation.)

One example of pronunciation software is "Streaming Speech," which was designed to help upper-intermediate and advanced learners with listening and pronunciation. There is a CD-ROM and a student's book (Cauldwell, 2003), which can be used independently or with a class. Students hear samples of British English utterances, record their own speech, and compare it to the models on the CD. At the Web site (www.speechinaction.com), there are downloadable resources, including scripts and communicative activities.

Students can get feedback from the teacher on their speaking by using modern technology too. For years, teachers have had students record their speech onto audiocassettes. The teacher typically listens to the audiotapes and then provides individualized feedback to the learners. You can also set up audiotape "swaps," in which each learner records an audio message to a classmate and pairs of students exchange tapes.

A more convenient modern technology, according to Chan (2003) is the free Internet player-recorder called PureVoice: "Instead of typing a text, students record their voices using a computer's microphone. The resulting sound file can be attached to any email" (Chan, 2003, p. 55). The students and teacher must all have the PureVoice software in order to exchange spoken messages, but the technological process can be more convenient than exchanging audiocassettes.

Chat rooms are parts of Web sites where the users can interact with one another. It used to be the case that such "conversations" were typed, but now the technology allows for voiced chats, where students can actually converse with other English learners and/or with a teacher. There is some evidence (Jepson, 2002) that communicating in voiced chat rooms gives learners many opportunities to negotiate for meaning, particularly as they try to understand one another's pronunciation. One Web site where learners can participate in voiced chats is www.englishtown.com.

A **corpus** is a body of computerized text stored in an electronic database. It may be based on written language or transcripts of spoken language. **Corpora** (the Latin plural) are collections of text. They provide useful databases for teachers and learners to investigate how language is actually used. Corpora can be electronically searched for particular grammatical structures, vocabulary items, idiomatic expressions, and so on.

One well-known corpus of spoken English is **CANCODE**–the Cambridge-Nottingham Corpus of Discourse in English. This corpus was built by a research team at the University of Nottingham, with funding from Cambridge University Press. Several samples from the corpus are available in *Exploring Spoken English* by Carter and McCarthy (1997), two of the researchers. CANCODE consists of five million words of conversation, including examples of narratives, service encounters (e.g., at the post office, ordering food in a restaurant), debates and arguments, and many other types of modern spoken English interactions.

Another very useful corpus is MICASE–the Michigan Corpus of Academic Spoken English. This corpus currently consists of over 150 transcripts with nearly two million words. This corpus can be searched for free by anyone who visits the Web site, which provides search tips and classroom worksheets for teaching English. It also explains the transcription conventions used. The speakers are both male and female students, who are native and non-native speakers of English, in graduate and undergraduate courses.

Concordances are computer programs that locate and highlight words or patterns in corpora. Programs such as Monoconc electronically search the database to find items designated by the program user. Concordancing makes it easy for teachers and researchers to see how language structures and vocabulary are really used in natural speech.

How can English teachers use a concordancing program with a corpus in teaching speaking and pronunciation? Carter and McCarthy (1997) provide a good example from CANCODE:

Example 2

Activity

English has a system of tags which speakers can put at the end of what they say. For example:

You're French, *aren't you?*
He's coming tonight, *is he?*

What do you think these tags are for? Make notes and/or discuss with a partner why you think speakers use tags. Are there other types of tags apart from the two types in the examples above?

Exploring Spoken English (Carter and McCarthy, 1997, p. 42)

The unit contains a transcript of a conversation between two old friends. Both are males in their forties. The conversation was recorded on a warm evening in the garden of a village pub in England.

Example 3

Speakers and setting

<S 01> male (40s)
<S 02> male (40s)

Two old friends who haven't seen each other for a few years are 'catching up' with each other. They are in a village pub garden on an exceptionally hot summer's evening, talking about <S 01>'s children.

Transcript

1	<S 01>	Are you still playing er
2	<S 02>	└Gui-tar
3	<S 01>	Irish music, yeah
4	<S 02>	No I don't play very much now, no, not at all
5	<S 01>	└I thought you were touring the

```
 6              country at one point
 7  <S 02>      [laughs] No, I er ... we go, we listen to it quite a lot, every time we
 8              go to Ireland we erm, you know, seek out good musicians and er do
 9              quite a lot of listening and of course we still buy a lot of records,
10              bought a lot of records over the last few years, but erm, there's not
11              actually anybody to play with around here, you know [<S 01> mm]
12              there's a there's a session every Sunday night in Cambridge in a pub
13              and that's erm about it ... do you still listen to Scottish music?
14  <S 01>      Ver ... since this pair have arrived [<S 02> mm] very very little, cos
15              you just don't have the time, and with the new house, and with the
16              garden [<S 02> Mm] occasionally I take fits of putting stuff on, not as
17              much as before
18  <S 02>      They do I s'pose take up a lot of time, don't they, kids?
19  <S 01>                                              ⌊They take up a lot
20              of, I mean, normally, you get, if you're lucky they're all tucked up in
21              bed by eight-thirty [<S 02> mm] ... that's if you're lucky, and then er
22  <S 02>      Do they sleep all night without erm waking up, did they wake up last
23              night, they didn't [<S 01> no] did they, no, [<S 02> no] didn't hear
24              a thing
25  <S 01>      Jamie normally, you put him in his cot and he's ... he's gone
26              [<S 02> mm] he sleeps he's very good at sleeping [<S 02> mm]
27              Thomas is a bit of a pain [<S 02> ah] all sorts of things frighten him,
28              you know [<S 02> yeah] wakes up with nightmares and that
29              [<S 02> does he] yeah some nights we change beds about three or
30              four times, he comes into our bed and there's not enough room and
31              so I go into his bed and he comes back in so to my bed and his bed
32              and chopping and changing
33  <S 02>      It's extraordinary to think they have bad dreams, well, I suppose they
34              dream of images they've seen during the day, probably dream of that
35              bloomin' duck or something
36  <S 01>      Or it just might be a car, noisy car going past the window or
37              something, wakes them up
38  <S 02>      Mm ... it's going to be hot tonight ... in bed, isn't it
39  <S 01>      Mm
```

Exploring Spoken English (Carter and McCarthy, 1997, pp. 42-43)

Reflection

What use could a teacher make of a corpus like CANCODE or MICASE?
Think of two or three ways you could use such a corpus to help you plan
a speaking lesson, or design speaking-related activities for your students.

At the end of the transcript, the authors provide this helpful chart
showing all the tag questions used in the conversation.

Example 4

Comments on activity

Tags in this extract:

l.18	They do I s'pose take up a lot of time,	don't they, kids?
ll.22–23	Did they wake up last night	they didn't [no]
ll.28–29	Wakes up with nightmares and that	\<S 02\> does he
l.38	It's going to be hot tonight ... in bed,	isn't it

Exploring Spoken English (Carter and McCarthy, 1997, p. 45)

The authors then comment on tag questions in spoken English. They use the data from the corpus transcript to illustrate their points:

Example 5

Points to note:

Tags have a very strong INTERACTIONAL effect in the conversation, reinforcing intimacy and informality. In the first case (l.18), the tag is followed by a lexical repetition (with *kids*) of the subject pronoun *they*. This is an example of a TAIL. Tails are frequent when speakers are commenting and evaluating states of affairs, and often accompany tags.

In l.23, the speaker answers his own question (*they didn't*) and adds a checking tag (*did they*). Speakers often use tags to check or confirm information in this way.

In l.29, note that tags often occur in the listener's response, to express the listener's reaction, or just to provide an acknowledgement or BACK-CHANNEL.

In l.38, the speaker assumes agreement on the part of the listener, and signals this assumption with the tag.

Exploring Spoken English (Carter and McCarthy, 1997, p. 46)

The Internet can also provide learners with rich sources of input, both by reading and by listening. Students can find interesting authentic materials on the Internet, in the form of news, weather reports, songs in English, blogs (online personal journals), sports reports, and so on. These texts consist of varied grammatical structures and wide-ranging vocabulary, which the students hear or read in context. You can give your students tasks based on finding particular information on the Internet. They can then report on their search orally to the class at the next session. Even beginning students and false beginners can benefit from the Internet information searches, especially if you have them work in pairs or teams.

Finally, there are now many Web sites that actually teach students about speaking and especially about pronunciation. Others provide teachers with information about helping learners improve their pronunciation. For example, at www.sunburstmedia.com, both teachers and learners can find useful resources, including accent reduction tools for learners, based on audio and videotapes. A Web site at Georgia State University provides links to many other sites that teachers will find helpful. (Visit www.gsu.edu/~esljmm/ss/furtherreading.htm for more information.)

In summary, modern technology offers English teachers many ways to help learners listen to, interact in, and investigate English. The use of technology can be especially helpful in EFL contexts, since it can enhance students' opportunities to hear and read authentic, interesting discourse. Computer-based resources can also provide teachers with quick access to lesson plans, reference materials, and classroom activities for teaching pronunciation.

9. Conclusion

In this chapter, we have considered some of the key issues in teaching speaking. Among the many challenges teachers face are working with large groups and multi-level classes, encouraging reticent students to speak in class, and helping dominating students to participate appropriately. We considered the role of students' first language use in the speaking classroom, and concluded that using the L1 can in fact help promote participation and possibly language learning. In discussing language learning styles and strategies, we saw a relationship between impulsive and reflective learning styles and the tendency to speak out or hold back in class discussions. We briefly examined some issues related to the treatment of learners' oral errors. And to conclude, we examined the possible contributions of technological advances, particularly in teaching pronunciation and providing students with on-line speaking opportunities.

 Further readings

Carter, R. and M. McCarthy. 1997. *Exploring Spoken English*. Cambridge: Cambridge University Press.

> This book is based on selections from CANCODE, a corpus of modern spoken English. The book contains a helpful glossary and twenty units based on transcripts of actual, unscripted conversations. Each unit contains an activity, a short description of the speakers and the setting, and a brief transcript, which is followed by a general commentary as well as line-by-line commentary and suggestions for further reading.

TESOL Quarterly. Volume 37, Number 3, Autumn 2003.

This special issue is an outstanding source of information about using corpora in English teaching. It includes a review of useful Web sites and information on concordancers.

Helpful Web sites

The University of Michigan's Corpus of Spoken Academic Discourse (www.lsa.umich.edu/eli/micase/micase_materials.htm)

This Web site provides a variety of authentic speech samples from postsecondary academic settings.

The Cambridge-Nottingham Corpus of Discourse in English (www.cup.cam.ac.uk/elt/reference/cancode.htm)

This Web site is an excellent resource for authentic samples of modern spoken British English.

References

Allwright, D. and K.M. Bailey. 1991. *Focus on the Language Classroom: An Introduction to Classroom Research for Language Teachers.* Cambridge: Cambridge University Press.

Allwright, R.L. 1980. Turns, Topics and Tasks: Patterns of Participation in Language Learning and Teaching. In D. Larsen-Freeman (ed.), *Discourse Analysis and Second Language Research.* Rowley, MA: Newbury House Publishers, 165-187.

Brooks, F. B. and R. Donato. 1994. Vygotskyan Approaches to Understanding Foreign Language Learner Discourse During Communicative Tasks. *Hispania,* 77: 262–274.

Brown, H.D. 1994. *Principles of Language Learning and Teaching* (3rd ed.). Englewood Cliffs, NJ: Prentice-Hall Regents.

Brown, J.D. 1980. Newly Placed Students Versus Continuing Students: Comparing Proficiency. In J.C. Fisher, M.A. Clark, and J. Schachter (eds.). *On TESOL '80 Building Bridges: Research and Practice in Teaching English as a Second Language.* Washington, DC: TESOL, 111-119.

Carter, R. and M. McCarthy. 1997. *Exploring Spoken English.* Cambridge: Cambridge University Press.

Cauldwell, R. 2003. *Streaming Speech: Listening and Pronunciation for Advanced Learners of English–Student's Book.* Birmingham, UK: speechinaction.

Chan, M. 2003. Technology and the Teaching of Oral Skills. *The CATESOL Journal* 15 (1): 51–56.

Christison, M.A. 2003. Learning Styles and Strategies. In D. Nunan (ed.), *Practical English Language Teaching.* New York, NY: McGraw-Hill, 267–288.

Hartmann, P. and L. Blass. 2000. *Quest: Listening and Speaking in the Academic World, Book 3.* Boston: McGraw-Hill.

Hughes, A. 1989. *Testing for Language Teachers.* Cambridge: Cambridge University Press.

Jepson, K. 2002. E-chat: Conversational repair moves between L2 speakers in Internet text and voice chat. Unpublished paper. Monterey Institute for International Studies, Monterey, California.

Kinsella, K. 1995. Understanding and Empowering Diverse Learners. In J. Reid (ed.), *Learning Styles in the ESL/EFL Classroom.* Boston, MA: Heinle/Thomson, 24–31.

LoCastro, V. 2001. Large Classes and Student Learning. *TESOL Quarterly,* 35(3): 493–496.

McCarthy, M. and S. Walsh. 2003. Discourse. In D. Nunan (ed.), *Practical English Language Teaching.* New York, NY: McGraw-Hill, 173–195.

Moholt, G. 1988. Computer Assisted Instruction in Pronunciation for Chinese Speakers of American English. *TESOL Quarterly* 22(1): 91–111.

Murphy, J. 2003. Pronunciation. In D. Nunan (ed.), *Practical English Language Teaching.* New York, NY: McGraw-Hill, 111–128.

Nunan, D. 2005. *Practical English Language Teaching: Grammar.* New York, NY: McGraw-Hill ESL/ELT.

Sarwar, Z. 2001. Innovations in Large Classes in Pakistan. *TESOL Quarterly,* 35(3): 497–500.

Shamim, F. 1996. In or Out of the Action Zone: Location as a Feature of Interaction in Large ESL Classes in Pakistan. In K.M. Bailey and D. Nunan (eds.), *Voices from the Language Classroom: Qualitative Research in Second Language Education.* New York: Cambridge University Press, 123–144.

Storch, N. and G. Wigglesworth. 2003. Is There a Role for the Use of the L1 in an L2 Setting? *TESOL Quarterly,* 37(4): 760–770.

Swain, M. and S. Lapkin. 2000. Task-based Second Language Learning: The Uses of the First Language. *Language Teaching Research,* 4: 251–274.

Tsui, A.B.M. 1996. Reticence and Anxiety in Second Language Learning. In K.M. Bailey and D. Nunan (eds.), *Voices from the Language Classroom: Qualitative Research in Second Language Education.* New York, NY: Cambridge University Press, 148–164.

Willing, K. 1987. *Learning Styles in Adult Migrant Education.* Sydney: National Centre for English Language Teaching and Research.

Glossary

accuracy – the ability to speak properly–that is, selecting the correct words and expressions to convey the intended meaning, as well as using the grammatical patterns of English correctly; control over "the linguistic code;" the ability to apply the rules of the language

achievement tests – tests used at the end of a course of instruction to see if students have learned the skills and content covered in that class

affricates – the segmental phonemes that consist of a stop followed immediately by a fricative, such as the /ǰ/ sound at the beginning and end of the word *judge,* and the /č/ at the beginning and end of the word *church*

alveolar ridge – the uneven surface on the roof of your mouth just behind your upper front teeth

analytic ratings – in testing speaking, speech scoring systems in which the abilities underlying the speaking skill have been analyzed and the test-takers are evaluated on how well they perform the various subskills (fluency, pronunciation, grammar, etc.)

Audiolingual Method (ALM) – a language teaching method based on the notion that learning another language is a matter of acquiring new linguistic habits through drill and practice

back-channeling – words or utterances from the listener that show the speaker that the listener is attending to what he or she is saying

backward build-up – (also called "back-chaining") a technique in which the instructor starts at the end of a long sentence and gradually adds phrases, so that students will be able to recall and reproduce the utterance

bidding for a turn – verbal and/or nonverbal signals that a participant in a lesson uses to indicate in some way that he or she wishes to speak

bound morphemes – morphemes that are always connected to words (such as *–ing, -tion, un-,* or *–s*)

CANCODE – a well-known corpus of spoken English, the Cambridge-Nottingham Corpus of Discourse in English

chat rooms – online environments in which computer users can interact with others, either by speaking (in voiced chat rooms) or by typing

choral repetition – having the students speak in unison while repeating an utterance

clarification request – moves by which "one speaker seeks assistance in understanding the other speaker's preceding utterance through questions…, statements such as *I don't understand,* or imperatives such as *Please repeat*" (Pica, Young, and Doughty, 1987, p. 740)

cloze test – a written text of at least a paragraph in length from which words have been deleted; the test taker must fill in each blank with a word that is grammatical and that makes sense

cocktail party technique – a procedure in which the learners stand and talk briefly with different people and then move on to talk to someone new, as if they were at a social gathering

coherence – "the relationships which link the meanings of utterance in a discourse" (Richards, Platt, and Weber, 1985, p. 45); how a text is constructed, including reliance on background knowledge

cohesion – "the grammatical and/or lexical relationship between the different parts of a sentence" (Richards, Platt, and Weber, 1985, p. 45), including reference, repetition, synonyms, and so on

communication strategies – verbal and/or nonverbal procedures used to compensate for gaps in speaking competence

communicative competence – the ability to interact successfully with other speakers using linguistic competence, sociolinguistic competence, discourse competence, and strategic competence

Communicative Language Teaching (CLT) – a language teaching method based on interaction in the target language

comprehensible input – language the learner hears or reads and can understand

comprehension check – "moves by which one speaker attempts to determine whether the other speaker has understood a preceding message" (Pica, Young, and Doughty, 1987, p. 740)

concordances – computer programs which locate and highlight words or patterns in corpora

confirmation check – "moves by which one speaker seeks confirmation of the other's preceding utterance through repetition, with rising intonation" of the preceding utterance (Pica, Young, and Doughty 1987, p. 740)

contact assignments – a type of short, focused interview task in which the language learners are obliged to have contact with speakers of the target language

contingent – turns in natural conversations are contingent in that they depend on previous turns as the topics evolve

contracted forms – shortened nouns/pronouns and verbs used in speaking

contrastive analysis – a systematic comparison of the students' first language with English to determine the differences that will need attention during instruction

conversational cloze test – a cloze passage for which the original text is the transcript of an actual conversation in which some words have been replaced by blank lines

corpus – a collection of texts (either from spoken or written discourse) saved in an electronic database

dependent clause – a clause that is not grammatical on its own and must be attached to an independent clause to be a complete grammatical sentence

diagnostic tests – tests used to see what students already know and what they still need to learn in terms of the syllabus of a particular course

Direct Method – a language teaching method that uses only the target language and focuses on everyday vocabulary and expressions

direct test of speaking – procedure in which the learners actually speak the target language, interacting with the test administrator and generating novel utterances

discourse competence – how sentence elements are tied together, which includes both cohesion and coherence

distinctive feature – a certain characteristic of a sound (such as voicing) that distinguishes it from another similar sound

English as a foreign language (EFL) – the teaching, learning, and use of English in contexts and communities where it is not a major medium of communication

English as a second language (ESL) – the teaching, learning, and use of English in contexts and communities where it is a major medium of communication, such as in Britain, Canada, New Zealand, Australia, and the United States

extemporaneous speaking – public speaking with preparation, often with brief notes

false beginners – students who have studied English but have not had an opportunity to speak it extensively and thus lack fluency, confidence, breadth of vocabulary, or easy mental access to grammar rules to apply when they are speaking

fluency – the capacity to speak fluidly, confidently, and at a rate consistent with the norms of the relevant native speech community; speaking rapidly and smoothly, but not necessarily grammatically

formulae – short stretches of language that learners memorize in context without breaking them down into their separate grammatical elements

free morphemes – units of language that can stand on their own and convey meaning, i.e., individual words

fricative – consonants produced through friction, such as /f/ and /v/ and /s/

functions (also called **speech acts**) – things we do through language (for example, 'introducing yourself,' 'ordering food and drink,' 'comparing prices,' 'talking about likes and dislikes')

glides – sounds that serve as transitions between two vowel sounds, during which the vocal tract is only slightly constricted, as /w/ and /y/ in English

Grammar-translation Method – a language teaching method in which students are taught to analyze grammar and to translate (usually in writing) from one language to another

grapheme – a written unit of language (for instance, a letter in an alphabetic writing system)

groupwork – three or more students working together in the target language

guided conversation – (also called **controlled conversation**) a conversation in which the students are given a framework within which to build their sentences, but "the actual choice of what they will say is left up to them" (Allen and Valette, 1977, p. 231)

holistic ratings – a scoring system in which a speech sample is given one overall evaluation, which may be a rating or a designation

impromptu speaking – spontaneous public speaking without preparation

impulsive learners – those who will speak out quickly, perhaps without much concern for accuracy

independent clauses – full sentences that can stand alone in writing, and typically have a subject and a verb marked for tense

indirect test of speaking – a test in which the test-takers do not speak (such as a conversational cloze test)

information gap tasks – activities in which learners must use the target language to convey information known to them but not to their speaking partners

input – language which a learner hears or receives

inside-outside circle – a technique for giving students the chance to repeat a conversation or interview with several new people, in order to build fluency and confidence

instructional impact (or **washback**) – the effect a test has on teaching and learning

intake – that subset of the input which learners notice, find helpful, and can learn from

interaction – two or more people communicating with one another

interlocutor – the person someone is talking to

interpersonal speech – communication for social purposes, including establishing and maintaining social relationships

interviews – structured or semi-structured sequences of questions intended to elicit particular information from the people answering the questions

intonation – in spoken language, variations in pitch, stress, and rhythm that convey meaning above and beyond the words and structures used

language classroom anxiety – the situationally triggered anxiousness that learners experience when they try to interact in the target language during lessons

learning styles – "natural, habitual, and preferred ways of absorbing, processing and retaining new information and skills" (Kinsella, 1995, p. 171)

linguistic competence – control over the grammar, words, and sounds of a language

manipulables – things you can manipulate in a language lesson, including commercial products, such as Legos and Cuisenaire Rods

manner of articulation – how sounds are produced, particularly consonants

metalanguage – language used to talk about language

MICASE – the Michigan Corpus of Academic Spoken English, consisting of over 150 transcripts

mitigation – various linguistic means of softening a message

modality – refers to the medium of the language (whether it is aural/oral or written)

monitoring – the process of learners checking or attending to what they say or write, based on rules they have already learned

morphemes – units of meaning that are either "free" (words that can stand alone) or "bound" (grammatical markers that must be attached to words such as *–ing* or *–ed*)

multi-level classes – classes in which there are noticeable differences in the various students' proficiency levels

needs assessment – a systematic process for determining learners' needs and goals, in order to design an appropriate syllabus or modify an existing syllabus

notice the gap – a learner's realization that the way he is saying something in the target language differs from the way native or proficient speakers say it

objective scoring – test marking that does not involve any judgment during the scoring process (i.e., it can be done by a computer or an untrained person using a scoring key)

output – a learner's speech or writing in the target language

pairwork – two students working together to complete a task or exercise using the target language

personalization – creating learning opportunities in which learners are encouraged to contribute their own ideas, feeling, and attitudes; designing tasks closely related to the learners' lives and interests.

phoneme – a divisible unit of sound that distinguishes meaning

phrase – two or more words that function as a unit, but unlike clauses, do not have a subject or a verb marked for tense (e.g., a prepositional phrase or infinitive phrase)

placement tests – tests given as learners enter a program of instruction to see what level class they should join

place of articulation – where in the vocal tract (the mouth, lips, and throat) speech sounds are actually produced, especially consonants

practicality – a quality of a test or other assessment procedure in terms of feasibility (i.e., it can only be useful if it does not make unreasonable demands on resources, including time, money, and personnel)

pre-teach – to teach structures, speech acts, or vocabulary items before an activity, in anticipation that the students will need to use them during the activity

primary trait scoring – a scoring procedure in which students are evaluated on the one particular characteristic (i.e., the primary trait) which is being emphasized in the speaking task

productive skills – speaking and writing (in which language is produced by the learners)

productive vocabulary – (also called "active vocabulary") those parts of learners' English vocabulary that they can use when speaking or writing

progress tests – tests used during a course to see how well students have mastered particular parts of the material covered up to that point

pronunciation software – computer programs, diskettes, and CDs designed to help language learners improve their pronunciation in the target language

proposition – the basic meaning(s) of a sentence or utterance; the concepts or ideas it conveys

receptive skills – reading or listening (in which language is directed at the learners)

receptive vocabulary – (also called "passive vocabulary") those parts of learners' English vocabulary that they recognize and can interpret in reading or listening, even if they can't use them productively in speaking or writing

reduced speech – the tendency of sounds to blend together, especially in casual conversation

reductions – phonological processes in which sounds are lost or muffled (e.g., when *little* is pronounced as "lil")

reflective learners – learners who prefer to think about their answers or comments before speaking in class

register – degrees of formality and informality in both spoken and written language

reliability – in testing, the consistency of a measurement

role-play – a classroom procedure in which learners play a part, either pretending to be someone else, and using information provided by the teacher or the textbook, or based on their own ideas or feeling

scavenger hunt – an activity in which teams of people compete to see who can collect a specified assortment of odd items most quickly–usually by asking people for them

segmental phonemes – consonants and vowels (i.e., phonemes that can be segmented)

self-initiated turn – when a student seeks, takes, or makes an opportunity to talk in class

semi-direct tests – oral tests in which students actually speak (that is, they produce oral language) but don't interact in a conversation, interview, or role-play; the test-takers listen to a recorded voice, and respond by talking to a recording device

sentence repetition – an assessment procedure in which the learner repeats aloud after the teacher a sentence selected to represent problem areas in pronunciation or grammar

simulations – somewhat elaborate role-play scenarios that demonstrate "reality of function in a simulated and structured environment" (Jones, 1982, p. 5)

sociolinguistic competence – the ability to use language appropriately in various contexts

speaking – the productive aural/oral skill

speech acts (or **functions**) – the use of language in recognizable ways to get things done

speech events – situated, identifiable, and somewhat predictable genres of spoken language associated with a certain context

Spoonerism – a typical speaking glitch named after Dr. Spooner, a famous British orator, who would sometimes switch his segmental phonemes and say things like "the queer old dean" when he meant to say "the dear old queen"

strategic competence – the learner's ability to use language strategies to compensate for gaps in linguistic skills and knowledge

style shifting – a change in style (to be more or less formal) in either speech or writing

suprasegmental phonemes – stress, rhythm, pitch, and intonation

syllables – parts of words that can be either open (ending with a vowel), or closed (ending with a consonant)

syllabus – the subcomponent of a curriculum that sets out the content to be covered by a textbook, a program, or a course of study

tango seating – a simple pair seating arrangement designed to force people to use oral communication during information gap tasks that involve drawing pictures, following maps, or creating designs or structures from verbal descriptions; the two students are seated facing in opposite directions and their right shoulders (or left shoulders) are together

target language – the language the students are trying to learn

teacher-fronted lessons – lessons in which the teacher manages the turn-taking, nominates most of the topics, and generally controls the discourse, often from the front of the classroom

text – a stretch of language, whether written or spoken

Total Physical Response (TPR) – an input-based teaching method in which language learners respond physically to commands or descriptions given in the target language

transactional speech – communicating to get something done, such as the exchange of goods and/or services

turn overlaps – simultaneous speech which occurs when two people or more speak at the same time in the same conversation

utterances – things that people say

validity – the quality of a test to measure what it is intended to measure

voicing – the situation in which the vocal cords are vibrating when speech is produced

wait-time – the length of time a teacher will wait for a student to respond, after the teacher has posed a task, issued a command, or asked a question

washback (or **instructional impact**) – the effect a test has on teaching and learning

References

Allen, E.D. and R.M. Valette. 1977. *Classroom Techniques: Foreign Languages and English as a Second Language.* New York, NY: Harcourt Brace Jovanovich, Inc.

Kinsella, K. 1995. Understanding and Empowering Diverse Learners. In J. Reid (ed.), *Learning Styles in the ESL/EFL Classroom.* Boston: Heinle/Thomson, 24–31

Pica, T., R. Young., and C. Doughty. 1987. The Impact of Interaction on Comprehension. *TESOL Quarterly,* 21(4): 737–758.

Richards, J., J. Platt, and H. Weber. 1985. *Longman Dictionary of Applied Linguistics.* London: Longman.

Index

Credits